Successful Women Speak Differently

VALORIE BURTON

HARVEST HOUSE PUBLISHERS
EUGENE, OREGON

Cover by Harvest House Publishers

Cover photo © Michele Mabie—Everything Lovely Photography

Makeup by Kym Lee

Valorie Burton is represented by Alive Literary Agency, 7680 Goddard Street, Ste #200, Colorado Springs, CO 80920. www.aliveliterary.com.

The personal stories in this book are composite accounts based on the author's experiences and constructed for purposes of illustration only. Where individuals may be identifiable, they have granted the author and the publisher the right to use their names, stories, and/or facts of their lives.

SUCCESSFUL WOMEN SPEAK DIFFERENTLY

Copyright © 2016 by Valorie Burton
Published by Harvest House Publishers
Eugene, Oregon 97402
www.harvesthousepublishers.com

ISBN 978-0-7369-5680-2 (pbk.)
ISBN 978-0-7369-5681-9 (eBook)

Library of Congress Cataloging-in-Publication Data
Names: Burton, Valorie, 1973- author.
Title: Successful women speak differently / Valorie Burton.
Description: Eugene, Oregon : Harvest House Publishers, 2016.
Identifiers: LCCN 2016031236 (print) | LCCN 2016033046 (ebook) | ISBN 9780736956802 (pbk.) | ISBN 9780736956819 ()
Subjects: LCSH: Christian women—Religious life. | Success—Religious aspects—Christianity. | Oral communication—Religious aspects—Christianity.
Classification: LCC BV4527 .B878 2016 (print) | LCC BV4527 (ebook) | DDC 248.8/43—dc23
LC record available at https://lccn.loc.gov/2016031236

Printed in the United States of America

18 19 20 21 22 23 24 / BP-SK / 10 9

Also by Valorie Burton

Successful Women Think Differently

Happy Women Live Better

Get Unstuck, Be Unstoppable

Start Here, Start Now

To Sophie and Addie:

I am proud of you for the enthusiasm, kindness, and hard work that make you successful girls. And I am excited about the successful women I believe you will become.

I love you,
B-Mom

ACKNOWLEDGMENTS

Writing a book is just one segment of the journey to getting it into your hands. The journey is more like a relay race in which many team members swiftly carry the baton that eventually reaches the finish line. I am grateful for the team of people who helped bring this book to fruition:

My editor, Kathleen Kerr. Your enthusiasm for my message, your thoughtful editing style, and calm, encouraging spirit are powerful and energizing. Thank you for the care and zest with which you tackled this project. I appreciate you so very much.

My literary agent, Andrea Heinecke, as well as the entire team at Alive Communications. Thank you for believing so firmly in my work and for your insights and guidance. It is a joy to work with you and hammer out ideas!

The entire team at Harvest House, including LaRae Weikert, Brad Moses, Bob Hawkins, Betty Fletcher, Christianne Debysingh, Jeff Marion, Aaron Dillon, Ken Lorenz, and Sharon Shook. Thank you for all you have done to bring my books to so many people around the world. It is a blessing to work with such dedicated, fun, conscientious people!

My publicist, Ben Laurro, of Pure Publicity. Thank for you being so persistent in promoting me and my message for more than a dozen years. I truly appreciate your tenacity, hard work, and spirit of service.

My team at Inspire Inc.—Wade, Alexis, and Leone Murray. What a blessing it is to work with people who have my back, love this work, and just happen to also be my family! It is amazing how God works. Thank you for working tirelessly every day to help me help others experience their potential. I love you.

My husband, Jeff, and our children, Sophia, Addison, and Alexander. Thank you for giving me the love and support that makes life so full of joy and meaning. And Jeff, thank you for always being a willing sounding board for all of my ideas (good and not so good), for late-night chats, and for enduring the stress of my deadlines! You are as patient and enthusiastic and understanding a husband as I could ever have asked for.

CONTENTS

A Good Start

Talk isn't cheap. It's your secret weapon.

Alisha and Erica are both artists whose work is creatively outstanding. They grew up in the same metro area with similar family backgrounds and identical access to opportunities. Their families did not have the contacts or networks to give the young women any particularly exceptional career start. But take a glimpse at how they've approached their careers and personal lives since the beginning, and you can piece together why one has been much more successful than the other.

Most people would say Erica has more raw talent. She also possesses a few more credentials, primarily as a result of having more formal education and training. She's the one who—on the surface—ought to be more successful.

Alisha's education was more adventurous. She studied abroad in college, exploring art and culture, but she never finished her degree. Driven by passion for her craft and the family financial crisis caused by her father's illness, Alisha left school. She took small jobs working around other artists and savoring every experience.

Erica, on several occasions, was introduced to people who could have opened doors for her career. But afraid of coming across as pushy or opportunistic, she never spoke up or voluntarily shared her aspirations or vision. On the occasions she was asked, she spoke cautiously of her vision, fearing that it didn't sound all that interesting or that her big goals came across as arrogant. This didn't doom her; it just didn't help her. Good opportunities have come her way, and it has occasionally looked like her art career would finally, really take off. But each time, she'd stall. One opportunity never seemed to flow to the next. They were one-offs, false starts.

Alisha, on the other hand, talked about her vision to pretty much anyone who would listen—and she did it in an easy, energetic way. She was sharing her passion, not selling something.

Now in her early forties, Alisha has seized every opportunity for her art, both nationally and internationally. Along the way, she's heard the whispers of plenty of naysayers who didn't think she was worthy. "Why her?" they ask. "She's good, but others are better." Alisha knew it was true: There were definitely others who were better. But Alisha never bought into the idea that her success was solely tied to her talent.

She shows up differently from other artists. She talks about her work differently. She engages in conversations differently. And it has made all the difference. In fact, her ability to "speak differently" has shaped more than her career. Her friendships are stronger because she is courageous and wholehearted in how she deals with people—telling the truth and setting expectations that minimize miscommunication and drama. Her finances have benefited because she isn't afraid to ask for what she wants—whether that's the fee for her work or a price break on a fabulous pair of shoes. An underlying clarity and boldness pushes Alisha a little closer to success than others, no matter what her goal.

Have you ever watched a woman with background and talents similar to your own find greater success? If so, you've probably wondered what made the difference. What caused her to meet her goals while you struggle in frustration, perhaps even feeling that the odds are stacked against you?

Successful women do at least two things differently from the average woman. First, they *think* differently in the face of both challenges and opportunities. Their thought patterns allow them to bounce back and show up in powerful ways in their lives. Second, they *speak* differently—both in everyday exchanges with the people they care about and in crucial conversations in the workplace. The confidence with which they communicate—their presence, credibility, and voice—can be far more influential than their talents or efforts.

It may not seem obvious at first, but the nuances of successful women's thoughts and speech lead to different ways of presenting themselves and their ideas to the world. As a result, they build trust, communicate confidently, and have a great deal of influence in their social and professional circles even when they are not in an official position of leadership. This book will share many of the habits these women possess and guide you to incorporate these habits into your own life.

We speak through more than just what we say. In this book, we'll explore the four primary forms of personal communication that can empower a boost in success and happiness:

1. **Voice**

   How your voice sounds impacts others' reactions to you—whether they follow you, believe you, interrupt you, or allow themselves to be influenced by you. It isn't always about what you say, but how you say it and how it is received.

2. **Words**

   The words you speak and don't speak matter. Being intentional about your word choice and conquering your fears to speak up when needed and remain silent when it is wise can mean the difference between success and failure.

3. **Body**

   Your body speaks even before you do. Understanding how your body projects confidence or lack thereof, warmth or coldness, anxiety or calm, is critical to your success and happiness.

4. **Actions**

   What you do or don't do speaks volumes about who you are. If your actions don't line up with your words, you'll undermine your own communication and send mixed messages that sabotage your best efforts.

Have you ever watched a woman with background and talents similar to your own find greater success?

Speak Life

King Solomon makes a bold statement in the book of Proverbs, saying simply, "Death and life are in the power of the tongue" (Proverbs 18:21 NKJV). We can speak life into situations purely by what we say and how we say it. Successful women know this and are intentional about how they show up and speak up—in relationships, at work, and in their everyday lives. It isn't always the big, bold statements. It is often the nuances of their approach that shift opportunities their way.

On the flip side, those who are less successful often speak death into situations, dreams, and relationships without even realizing they are doing so. If you can begin to see the ways in which you may have subtly sabotaged your own desires in the past, then with that knowledge, you have the power to entirely recast your future. You can do so by adjusting how you show up and speak up.

After more than 15 years of coaching women in almost every state in America and multiple foreign countries, and after studying the massive research that exists on the subject of happiness and success, I have seen firsthand that women who succeed at manifesting the desires of their heart have a few things in common. Likewise, I have also observed some commonalities among women who struggle to achieve and sustain authentic success and happiness. Can you relate to any of these?

The Successful Woman	The Average or Unsuccessful Woman
Accurately perceives her own abilities; aims high and sets goals that are truly the desires of her heart.	Underestimates her abilities; sells herself short; sets goals that are beneath her potential and the desires of her heart.
Speaks up, even in the face of fear or intimidation.	Holds back out of fear, insecurity, and doubt.
Tells the truth kindly, even when it is uncomfortable.	Beats around the bush, even telling lies to avoid disapproval, conflict, or discomfort.

The Successful Woman	The Average or Unsuccessful Woman
Shows up in an authentic way in all relationships.	Changes to fit a mold shaped by others; is easily swayed by opinion; lives for approval and praise.
Asks powerful questions of herself and others; gets clarity about the way forward.	Makes assumptions; doesn't seek clarity when hearing an answer she doesn't want.
Has the courage to make requests for what she wants and needs.	Accepts what is offered, even when it doesn't meet her needs and goals.
Knows when to remain silent; doesn't overshare or talk excessively; is discerning about who can be trusted.	Speaks from a place of insecurity to release nervous energy and avoid silence; overshares, even with people who do not have her best interests at heart.
Takes ownership; speaks in terms of solutions, not complaints.	Makes excuses; blames; complains without a focus on problem-solving.
Says no to good opportunities in favor of purposeful ones.	Focuses on what she doesn't have rather than what she does have.
Speaks truthfully yet kindly about herself; never puts herself down; receives compliments easily.	Bats down compliments; speaks of herself in negative terms; doesn't give herself credit for strengths, efforts, and good deeds.

My guess is that you already have some measure of success. After all, the kind of woman who picks up a book on success is typically already successful to some degree. But you know, deep down, that you've only scratched the surface of what's possible for you. You may often be praised for your accomplishments thus far, and yet you sense there is something more for you to do and be. Maybe you already know what the big goal is, but for some reason it feels elusive.

I believe our paths have crossed because your full potential does not have to remain elusive. The purpose of this book is to give you that edge—a boost that gets you moving to the next level in your personal and professional life. It is a level that brings you not just accomplishment, but greater happiness.

What It Means to Succeed

Whatever you assume I mean by the word *successful* in the book's title is what I am guessing you want more of in your life. That word motivated you. And that's good. Most people want success, whether they define it as having a happy family or climbing the corporate ladder or building a healthy bank account or fitting into a size six dress. But before I begin sharing concepts and strategies for success, let's make sure we agree on what success is.

As I define it, success is a harmony of purpose, resilience, and joy. When these three elements flow together, you will experience true success. Think of it this way: *Success is living your life's purpose and embracing resilience and joy as you do.*

Let's break this definition down further.

Purpose: Service Fulfills the Successful Woman

Purpose is about making a difference in the lives of people. In other words, you cannot live your life's purpose unless you are in some way serving others. Although our purpose often brings us joy, it is not about us. It is always about using our strengths in the service of others. Your purpose in life answers a simple question: How is someone's life better because she has crossed your path?

Your Maker endowed you with gifts, talents, passions, and experiences that are unique to you. If I could travel back in time and observe you at 4 years old or 14 years old, I would see traces of your uniqueness. Your strengths have been with you all along, and now it's time for you to use them. There is a greater impact for you to make, and now is the time to make it.

In 1999, while standing in a bookstore, I had an epiphany about my life's purpose: to inspire women to live fulfilling lives, and to do so through my writing and speaking. At the time I was running my own public relations firm, using my gifts and talents as a communicator, but I wasn't passionate about the work. My passion was lacking because those gifts were not being used for the purpose for which I was created: to serve women.

Maybe you can relate. You've got half the purpose formula right. You're using your gifts and talents, just not in a way that ignites your passion in service to others. Or maybe you're in the right place, serving those you are most passionate about, but you lack the opportunity to use your gifts and talents in the way you've always dreamed. It can be quite frustrating—and as we will learn in a few chapters, negative emotion generated by feelings like frustration can sabotage your ability to be successful. Living your purpose is not only what you're here for, but it also empowers you to succeed.

Resilience: Hope Sustains the Successful Woman

As you set out in pursuit of your dreams, you will inevitably face challenges, trials, and stumbling blocks along the way. A key to your success will be developing a critical skill that every truly successful woman possesses in abundance: resilience. Nothing is perhaps more important to actually achieving success than the ability to be resilient in the face of challenges. Whatever your vision for the future, the likelihood of obstacles on the path to that vision is almost certain.

This is where successful women excel. They think differently in the face of fear, failure, setbacks, and challenges. They say different things to themselves in the face of such obstacles. As you read, you will learn to become more self-aware about the thoughts that knock on the doorstep of your mind. You will learn to choose which ones to let in and entertain.

Joy: Happiness Empowers the Successful Woman

Joy empowers you to succeed. As Nehemiah 8:10 reminds us, "The joy of the Lord is your strength" (NKJV). Wherever you are on your life's journey, if you find a way to embrace this season and enjoy it, you will already have found some measure of success.

Joy is not just about what happens in life—the little boosts of positive emotion that come when something makes you happy for a moment. Yes, that bite of chocolate will make you happy for a moment, so, hey, savor it. But deeper joy comes from peace and love and knowing you are living the life you were meant to live. You can have all the little joy moments your heart can stand, but if you have to drag yourself out of bed in the morning to go to a job you dislike and come home to a contentious household every evening, you are not going to feel successful. Every truly successful woman seeks peace in her decisions, love in her relationships, and purpose in her life.

As women, we have a unique set of concerns and challenges to navigate on our path to success. We have unique societal expectations, ones that often tell us who we *should* be. But who we *want* to be may not fit into that box. I don't know what life is calling you to, but I know that if it's your purpose, you are uniquely equipped to fulfill that calling.

Success will quite likely look different for you than it does for the woman next door or even your mother or your sister. While we are all wired a bit differently, some basic foundations for happiness and success must be present. When it comes to educating yourself on what it will take for you to achieve your next level of success—living your purpose while embracing resilience and joy—you will benefit from a perspective that honors your uniqueness as a woman.

So here's the practical approach you'll find in this book:

- Real-life stories of real women, just like you, who have found that harmony of purpose, resilience, and joy that defines success. You'll learn from their failures and triumphs, and most importantly, their thought processes along the journey.

- Practical, relevant research, some of it surprising, about how successful women speak and approach life differently than the average woman. This research will equip and educate you with the tools and knowledge that can get you to your goals.

- Coaching questions to help you determine your next step. Successful women know that when you ask the right questions, you get the right answers. Throughout the book, you will find questions to help you gain clarity about who you are, where you're going, and how to get there.

- Spiritual insights to strengthen you for the journey. God made no mistakes when He created you. You were uniquely designed for success in your purpose. When you align your life with your strengths—those innate qualities you were gifted with—you will tap into a level of grace that empowers you to achieve things you could never accomplish in your strength alone. Throughout the book, you will be reminded of the power at work in you when you open yourself to His divine love and guidance.

A Note About Coaching

As you read, you'll see that I use the term *coaching* and provide you with coaching questions. Coaching is the process of asking thought-provoking questions and providing a safe space to explore the answers, empowering you to take action, learn, grow, and ultimately get moving toward your destination.

This is where transformation takes place. While the stories and research insights will inspire you and give you practical knowledge that you can apply to your everyday life, the coaching questions will give you clarity about which steps to take next. Do not skip over the questions. Refuse to hurry through this process. Instead, savor it. If you do, I guarantee that you will experience real change before you finish this book.

As your coach through these pages, my goal is to be a catalyst. I'm just a vessel here to get a message to you. What you do with that message is up to you. I believe the power lies within you to make changes and adjustments in your life that will lead you straight to your dreams. One step at a time, one day at a time, expand and explore your options. Take action. Notice what works and what doesn't, and then make adjustments. Take another step. That's coaching.

My ultimate goal is to help you develop the habit of coaching yourself. You won't always have another person there to coach you—or even a book to spark guidance and direction—but you will always have you. If you develop the skills to coach yourself, you will have a consistent advantage in life. Because your choices, the ones you make from here on out, will make the difference.

Valorie

PART 1

Think Differently So You Can Speak Differently

Uncover the Missing Piece

You Are Capable of Far More Than You Know

Uncover the Missing Piece

*Why talent and effort aren't enough
to move you to the next level*

Key Lessons

- Talent and effort aren't enough to propel you toward your goals.

- Your ability to communicate can mean the difference between success and failure.

- If you want to open doors of opportunity, you need to learn to speak differently.

O n paper, she looked amazing. A degree from the top university in the state. Experience that showcased her skills for the job. Volunteer work with kids. And her talent, while narrow in scope, was outstanding. She had come so close to landing the position a year earlier. Her resumé checked every box. Her bosses and bosses' bosses narrowed it to two candidates, and Kimberly was still in the running. In fact, when she found out the other candidate was Lisa, she suddenly felt even more confident the job was hers. She had more experience than Lisa, she'd put in more hours, and frankly, she was the more talented of the two. If you asked some coworkers, they'd probably admit that Lisa had average technical ability.

But throughout the interview process, their bosses had the feeling that Lisa could do the job, that she could bring people together, even boost morale—something the company had not even specified they were looking for but definitely needed. Upper management liked her attitude and loved her connection with colleagues. She was warm and engaging. She asked great questions. One member of the interview team said, "Talking to her just makes me get outside my box and think bigger." All of the pluses for Lisa were extras, not requirements for the job. They were not listed in the job requirements. You couldn't really see them on paper. On paper it seemed she was less qualified than Kimberly. But her resumé didn't account for her most valuable trait: her ability to connect.

Kimberly was disappointed but not discouraged. After all, the management position she wanted *everyone* wanted. It was a large company, and lots of people had applied for the job. She came in second for it, so with more effort and an extra year under her belt, she'd try again when another spot opened up the following year. When the time came, she was ready! She knew the drill, she'd been through the interview process before, and as far she could tell, many of the same people were applying again, which meant she'd already come out ahead of them the year before. Once again, she made it to the final interview round—just two remaining candidates. This time it was Kimberly and Chris. "I was so confident. I knew it was time," she shared with me later. But it wasn't. Chris, who unlike Lisa was just as qualified as Kimberly on paper, won over the decision makers with his authenticity. The feedback Kimberly got from a mentor later? "In the end, they connected with Chris. He is relatable and approachable."

This time, more than being disappointed, Kimberly was frustrated. She'd always believed that her talent and effort would take her where she wanted to go in life and in her career. That was a core belief. And here, no matter how hard she tried, how long she persevered, and how great her resumé looked, she couldn't seem to break through. She'd checked all the boxes, or so she thought.

But there was actually a box she had missed entirely. It was one that many women disregard or consider irrelevant—and it's the one that makes all the difference.

This is about how you show up in your world.

The Missing Piece

In all my years of teaching and learning about success, these are the most talked-about strategies I've come across: *Vision. Discipline. Singular focus. Perseverance. Talent. Effort. Having the right team. Goal setting. Resilience.* Perhaps they sound familiar to you too.

Now, don't misunderstand me here. All of those pieces of the success puzzle are relevant. However, there is a missing piece whose value is underestimated. In fact, with this single missing piece, you could completely undermine the greatest talent, effort, and goal setting. You could undo everything a fantastic team or stellar discipline can help you build. The missing piece in the success puzzle is often talked about separately from the others. It goes by different names: *Communication. Influence. Presence. Confidence. Personal branding. Connection.*

I like to call it your *voice*. It encompasses everything you communicate to yourself and about yourself. Your voice is how you speak to the world and how you speak to yourself—a filter through which all your beliefs are processed and presented to the world within you and the world around you. Your voice can sabotage the best talent and boost an average talent. It can speak to the heart of the man who is authentically right for you, and it can protect your heart by serving as a bold shield from one who would do you harm.

This is about how you show up in your world.

Successful women speak differently. And because they do, doors of opportunity—whether personal or professional—open more easily, quickly, and unexpectedly. That's what happened with Lisa and Chris, and it blindsided poor Kimberly. Kimberly had the talent and discipline, put forth the effort, set the goal, and even bounced back from disappointment. But it doesn't help to "check all the boxes" if a missing box never gets checked.

Your voice can sabotage the best talent and boost an average talent.

It seems almost unfair. And if you're experiencing it, that's the biggest frustration. *What am I doing wrong? Why am I not breaking through? How is it that someone with less talent is further along than I am?* These are great questions to ask, but be careful how you answer them. Refuse to play victim or to insist that the odds are stacked against you. Consider that maybe, just maybe, there is a gap you can close that will make these questions irrelevant to you in the future. You won't wonder why you're not breaking through if indeed you've broken through! The person with less talent won't be further along.

It's time to learn to use your voice in a different way.

You can connect wholeheartedly in your relationships.

You can speak with confidence about your needs and wants.

You can stop using your voice to beat yourself up for mistakes.

You can exude a presence that supports your highest goals.

It's time to find out how.

"I feel like I'm doing all the right things. Why am I not seeing the results?"

Are you missing the piece? Ask yourself these questions to find out:

- Does fear keep you from speaking up, sharing ideas, or asking for what you want?

- Do you sometimes find that people take what you said the wrong way or misunderstand your intentions?

- Have you found it difficult to develop a relationship with a strong mentor or successful colleagues who can help you move your goals forward?

- Do you often rehash what you wish you had said in a conversation because you failed to communicate authentically when the conversation occurred?

You Are Capable of Far More Than You Know

Why you must stop underestimating your abilities and step up to bigger possibilities.

Key Lessons

- Confidence leads to action, and action leads to greater confidence.

- Making smart decisions up front makes the path smoother overall.

- Bold moves lead to stellar destinations.

One of the most fascinating consistencies in research about men, women, and communication is the finding that as women, we have a tendency to underestimate our own potential. In one study, for example, after completing a test, women tended to think they fared worse than they actually did. Men, on the other hand, tended to think they did better than they actually did. In other studies, men and women both rated their performances better than they actually were, but men exaggerated the results at more than twice the rate women did. Researchers have even coined a term for this tendency in men. They call it "honest overconfidence."[1] And here's the thing: If you honestly think you are better than you are, you'll step up for opportunities even when you might not quite be qualified or ready. And while you won't get some of the opportunities, some you will! You will believe for more. You will communicate with more confidence, and other people will come to believe you are capable. Because you are exposed to opportunities, you

25

will learn key skills sooner than you would have if you had underestimated yourself and shied away from bigger possibilities.

You are capable of far more than you know. You have to believe that. Stop underestimating yourself. When you do, you will begin communicating your openness to a better life—in your relationships, career, finances, and even your health. Your faith will expand—and so will your success. I've learned this the hard way.

Looking back now, it sounds so ridiculous. A young woman, fresh out of graduate school before her twenty-second birthday with a master's degree in journalism. Solid grades. A ton of well-written, interesting news clips to her credit. A public relations internship in the governor's office and another in media relations for a professional hockey team, where she actually coordinated press conferences and worked on the team's television show. Articulate, thoughtful interview skills. And a list of public relations firms and media outlets she'd like to work for. There is just one problem: She doesn't reach out to even one of them for a job opportunity.

On this particular day, she polishes her resumé for the sixteenth time before writing another cover letter. She needs to find out whom to send it to at the firm. It's a really reputable company. They have offices all over the world and one where she now lives. Surely she would be perfect for an entry level assistant account executive position. But as she reads the position description, she estimates she has only about 80 percent of the required experience and skills. So she decides not to apply.

This is the thought that she hears: "They gave you a list of requirements. Your experience doesn't reflect this whole list. Why waste their time? They already stated what they want." She takes the list literally, as though there will be a penalty and punishment for applying without being able to check off everything on the list. Such precision has served her well at times and could actually make a public relations client quite happy, but in a job hunt, it is total self-sabotage. And it is rooted in something else that has the potential to derail her career in the future.

Not applying for the job is really an act of self-preservation. Deep down, her fear of rejection is so tremendous, she'd rather stick to applying for opportunities for which she is a shoo-in than risk being told she didn't make the cut. I have had plenty of time to analyze this young woman's issues and motives. That's because she is me.

Oh, how I wish I could go back and advise my younger self. I think of the moments during that job-searching period when I stared at a name, thinking, "I should reach out to that person." But I didn't.

What would I say to myself if I had the chance? "Someone is going to see your potential and be thrilled to hire you." "You don't need to be 100 percent qualified on paper to get the job. You need to just throw your hat in the ring! This is how it works in the real world."

I thought the issue was unique to the younger me until I began studying the research on the matter. And I discovered this:

- Women are more likely than men to underestimate their abilities.

- Women speak with less confidence about their accomplishments.

- Women are more likely to apply for jobs only when they meet all of the listed qualifications.

So it wasn't just me at a young age. It's many of us. And because we take this approach again and again, we end up making a series of less bold moves that lead us to less stellar destinations. We are talented but frustrated, working hard but not seeing rewards for our efforts.

The most successful women know what they bring to the table and what skills they still need to acquire. This knowledge makes them confident, and confidence compels them to act. By understanding their abilities and possibilities, these women become more successful than their peers.

*Your internal beliefs about yourself
directly influence your external success.*

Action, Confidence, Action

Lori started interviewing for jobs last year after she completed her bachelor's degree in business. She seemed insecure, struggling to speak accurately about her abilities. Her report to her parents after every interview was that she had "bombed," had done terribly, or should have answered the questions differently.

But to her own surprise, Lori eventually landed a coveted job as an analyst at a Fortune 500 company. Clearly her perception of her performance was not quite accurate. What finally gave her the edge?

Lori is not only super easy to like because she is authentic and friendly, but she is intelligent and a diligent worker. She had one more thing going for her: a willingness to seek and consider feedback. She shared her aspirations with family and friends of family. She reached out for guidance from people much further along in their careers. And she was willing to *act* on their advice. The very fact that she was willing to act is evidence that she had some measure of confidence.

Here's why I say that: Confidence is what stirs us to act, and action leads to greater confidence. Sometimes it is the confidence of others that gives us the courage to take the first steps. Our perceptions are not always accurate, so we need wise mentors who can help steer us in the direction of our possibilities. In Lori's case, her mentors' belief in her gave her the confidence she needed in her interviews. So when the time came to interview for the job she finally got, Lori was ready.

Your internal beliefs about yourself directly influence your external success. If you believe that you're not ready, not qualified, and not prepared, those beliefs will prevent you from taking chances and accepting opportunities. However, if you know yourself to be capable of learning new skills, you'll find yourself facing new challenges with confidence and a positive attitude.

Confidence leads to action. Building your confidence will help you move forward and take the next steps. If you believe you are capable, you act like it. Confidence perpetuates success.

Action creates belief. When you begin acting like you belong in a higher place, your emotions catch up. You believe more is possible. As a result, your actions line up with the belief. Even in small ways, this is powerful.

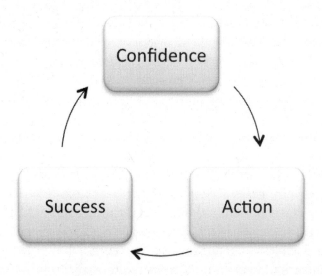

What action steps can you take today that will build your confidence? Brainstorm your own ideas for small steps that will increase your poise and self-assurance in a big way.

-
-
-
-
-
-
-
-
-
-

*Confidence is what stirs us to act, and action
leads to greater confidence.*

Stellar Starting Point

I wish I'd had the confidence to take action in the early years of my career. I was giving up before I even got started. Many women with similar talent and work ethic position themselves at a lesser starting point simply because they don't take those first steps. They underestimate their abilities, so they aim for less than they're really capable of. And that's exactly what they get! Years may pass before they become exasperated by operating in a place that is beneath where they actually desire to be.

"The most successful people make wise decisions early in life and manage those decisions for the rest of their lives." I heard leadership expert John Maxwell say this years ago, and it stuck with me. Whether in your relationships, career, financial abilities, health and fitness habits, or spiritual journey, starting strong makes the rest of your path easier.

Sound like a Success

*Your pattern of speech can predict
the likelihood of your success.*

The human voice is the organ of the soul.
HENRY WADSWORTH LONGFELLOW

Key Lessons

- Attractive-sounding voices get interrupted less often, influence decisions and ideas more, and command more attention.

- Your voice sounds different to others than to you, so truly hearing yourself is a critical step to improving the sound of your voice.

- Voice inflection, tone, and word speed all subconsciously communicate your insecurities or your authenticity.

It was the week before the Heisman Trophy was to be awarded. I sat waiting with anticipation to interview Charlie Ward, the superstar two-sport athlete from my undergraduate alma mater who would go on to capture the Heisman that year. As I sat in the lobby of Florida State University's athletic center, I ticked off my mental checklist: *Interview questions. Check. Notebook. Check.* I pressed record and the tiny red light glowed, confirming the recorder was all set to capture Charlie's every word. *Tape recorder. Check.*

As I sat in one of the cushioned chairs to wait for him to arrive from the locker room after practice, I tried to look relaxed and confident. Usually that wasn't too hard for me, but this was *Charlie Ward.* And it was 1994. In Tallahassee. He was a legend already, and it was still a month before FSU would take their first national championship. The anticipation was starting to make me a little anxious.

This was my first big interview, and I wanted it to be good. *Really good.* And waiting gave me too much time on my hands and I started overthinking. As my thoughts jumped from one thing to the next, I started second-guessing everything, including whether I looked calm and collected as I waited. I crossed my legs. Then decided that might come across as flirtatious. So I uncrossed them. I leaned back in the chair. Then decided that was a little too casual. I decided to scoot up to the edge of the seat and glance at my notes. I tested my recorder once again to make sure it was working. It was. I took a few deep breaths.

And then he walked up.

"Hi, Charlie," I greeted him.

"Are you Valorie?" he asked.

And so our conversation began. Small talk at first. Then I hit record and flipped the page on my notes.

That's when something went wrong. My recorder, the one I had tested twice while I was waiting on Charlie, suddenly stopped working. I started fumbling with it. Each time I hit the record button, the button popped back up.

Seriously, Val? I thought to myself. *You've been planning this interview for two weeks and now the recorder won't record?*

I tried to play it off like it was no big deal, but my mind started racing: *It's the end of the week. I have to get this story. Getting Charlie Ward for another interview before my deadline will be impossible.* I tried to continue the small talk while pressing the button over and over, but suddenly my voice didn't sound like its normal, even self. I started to stumble over my words.

He must have sensed the panic that was welling up inside because he then said exactly what I did not want to hear, something that indicated he could see right through my attempts to appear cool and confident. In a voice that sounded genuinely surprised and entirely encouraging, he gently uttered these words: "You're not nervous, are you?"

For a woman who likes to be in control, being called out as not having it totally together felt like a bright light shining on my insecurities.

I muttered, "Um. No, it's just my recorder is…it was working just a minute ago…" He smiled and offered to help with the tape recorder, and within a moment it was working again. The rest of the interview was fantastic.

My reaction that afternoon is one that you, too, have probably had at one time or another. The irony of trying to hide our anxiety is that it comes out anyway. And if our body language doesn't signal it, our voice certainly does. Our feelings show up in the words we say, how fast we say them, the steadiness of our voice, and even our pitch.

Your vocal essence can shape how others see you, what they believe about you, and the doors that ultimately open for you.

Vocal Essence

Your "vocal essence" is the quality of what others hear when you speak. It is the essence of what your voice expresses. And what your voice expresses emerges from the depths of your mind, soul, and spirit. The poet Henry Wadsworth Longfellow said, "The human voice is the organ of the soul." Like a musician expressing her art through an instrument, so we express the artistry of our thoughts and emotions through the voice. Happiness, anger, sadness, authority, warmth—all are conveyed in the power of your voice. Yet most of us never think much about that voice, or more specifically, our vocal essence.

I can hear what's going on by *listening*—not just to the words you use, but your pitch, speed, volume, and the clarity with which you speak those words. And when you choose to mask your emotion by speaking in a monotone voice, the people listening can perceive that you are not being authentic, that there is a wall between you and them. Even when you fake emotions, the mind of the listener can still perceive the lack of authenticity. You might not be able to pinpoint exactly what it is that speaker is faking, but within your own soul you get the sense that something is simply "off." If the voice is the organ of the soul, then it is the soul that perceives it best.

So just what can you do about that? Can you really make changes that will transform the sound of your voice?

Absolutely. It is possible to "sound like a success" just by making small tweaks in your everyday interactions and thoughts. In fact, to move to a higher level of success, it is absolutely necessary. Success is determined not just by talent and effort, but by your influence over others. That influence comes from your ability to communicate ideas, concepts, trust, credibility, and warmth. And your most basic element of communication is your *voice*.

Your "vocal essence" is the quality of
what others hear when you speak.

As you may have experienced, the way people perceive the essence of what you say and how you say it can open doors or close them, build relationships or diminish them. So if you want to achieve higher levels of success and happiness, start here: Improve your vocal essence, the quality of how your soul expresses itself in the world.

Your vocal essence can shape how others see you, what they believe about you, and the doors that ultimately open for you. So let's begin with this most basic concept of how successful women speak differently. I want to share tools to help you improve your vocal essence, build your influence, speak authentically and courageously, and communicate in a way that represents your highest purpose and vision.

If the voice is the organ of the soul, then it
is the soul that perceives it best.

Do You Upspeak?

One particularly persistent shift in inflection has occurred in American English over the last few decades, and it can undermine you when your goal is to speak with confidence. Maybe you've noticed it. It's called "upspeak."

In the United States, it is generally believed that this tendency originated out West. It's often associated with the Valley Girl speak that became popular in the 1980s, and it has latched on to communication styles among young people ever since. Researchers became curious about the tendency for Gen Xers to end statements with rising intonation so that a declarative statement sounds more like a question. Studies about the phenomenon gained media attention. Believe it or not, there is a scientific term for upspeak—*high-rising terminal*, or HRT for short.[1]

Rather than confidently make a statement, upspeak dramatically softens the statement by making it sound like a question, as though you are a bit uncertain. Young people are more likely to use upspeak than older adults, and women are more likely to use it than men. Women are often socialized to talk in ways that are less powerful, authoritative, and confident, according to Robin Lakoff, Ph.D., a professor of linguistics at University of California at Berkeley. What she describes as "rising intonation on declarative sentences" is a common aspect of what she calls "women's language."[2]

Consider each of these statements and say each one aloud while maintaining a consistent vocal tone all the way to the end. Then say the first statement aloud, but when you get to the last two or three words, allow your intonation to rise as though asking a question (notated in italics):

- You are having a difficult conversation with a friend who shared a confidence with someone without your permission. She is apologetic, but you are very disappointed and want to come to an agreement about how to move forward in your friendship:

  Upspeak: In the future, I am just asking that anything

we talk about, unless I specifically tell you it is okay to share, stays *between you and me*?

Confident: In the future, I am just asking that anything we talk about, unless I specifically tell you it is okay to share, stays between you and me.

- You are sitting in a meeting at work. You have an opinion or recommendation. Perhaps you have been asked to come with a solution. And you respond...

  Upspeak: I recommend that we proceed with *the first* option?

  Confident: I recommend that we proceed with the first option.

- You are in an interview for a new position for which you know you are qualified. You answer a question by highlighting a relevant piece of experience:

  Upspeak: In my last job, I was responsible for managing *the operating budget*?

  Confident: In my last job, I was responsible for managing the operating budget.

Why would you end a statement by making it sound like a question? If you fear the person you are talking to might disapprove or be offended, then changing your intonation to make the statement sound like a question is a way of asking for their approval. It sounds unsure. If your statement is a request, upspeak makes the request sound optional.

We can sabotage our own words simply by changing the tone of our voice, phrasing a clear statement as an uncertain question or request for permission. I am not suggesting that you need to speak forcefully or be demanding, but you must be intentional and authentic by making your statements statements. This not only conveys your confidence in what you say, but it also makes others feel more confident in you. Think about it. Do you feel more at ease handing over an important task to someone who sounds uncertain or someone who sounds sure of herself?

Own your statements. Own your ideas. Take credit for them and advocate for them. That doesn't mean you're not open to other people's ideas and making adjustments to your own after getting feedback. It is entirely possible to own your statements and remain flexible and open to additional possibilities.

Sound like a success just by making small tweaks in your everyday interactions and thoughts.

Questions That Are Meant as Statements

Another way you can sabotage your communication is the opposite of upspeak. It is phrasing statements as questions...and then pushing back on anyone who gives you the wrong answer! It looks something like this:

> Marie: Should we buy the brown pillow rather than the red one because the color will be a little softer next to the wall?
>
> Joy: No, I don't think so. The red complements the throw on the sofa better.
>
> Marie: Yeah, but there's nothing else red in the room.
>
> Joy: So it sounds like you want the brown?

Only ask the question if you actually want to hear what the other person has to say. Otherwise, you'll create frustration. Other people can actually begin to shut down, not bothering to respond to your questions because their answers are never valued. They learn that you don't want feedback, new information, or an opinion. You just want them to agree with you.

We can sabotage our own words simply by changing the tone of our voice.

Your Voice Is Shaped by Your Thoughts

One of the core principles of my book *Successful Women Think Differently* is the understanding that your thoughts create your actions. If you become aware of what you are saying to yourself about your situation, you can consciously decide if the thought is moving you toward your goals or further away. But your thoughts don't just lead you to take actions such as initiating a conversation or going back to school or opening your heart again after it's been broken. Your thoughts also shape the sound of your voice. Your voice is the external expression of your internal state.

If your internal state is anxious, for example, and you think danger may be imminent, your voice will reflect that anxiety. Your body responds to the thought of anxiety. It is basic physiology.

The sound of your voice is regulated by the vagus nerve, which is central to the parasympathetic nervous system. When the vagus nerve is stimulated, which can happen as a fight-or-flight response to anxiety-producing thoughts, the vocal cord muscles spasm. This can cause your voice to quiver or "sound nervous." Additionally, when stressed or nervous, you typically don't breathe deeply. As a result, you don't have the air that creates the pressure needed for a strong-sounding voice.

What can you do about it?

- Become aware of your thoughts and redirect counterproductive thoughts to productive ones. Instead of mulling over a counterproductive thought, intentionally redirect it by changing your environment, choosing a new thought, or engaging in an activity that gets your mind moving in a new direction.

- Exercise. Exercise purges negative energy.

- Practice. If there is something you need to say that makes you uncomfortable or anxious, or that you must present to a group, practice what you are going to say in advance. Even record it and listen to find the areas where you want to improve. Practice alleviates nervous energy.

- Hydrate. Hydration alleviates dry mouth. Drink water before or during important conversations.

- Talk it out. Choose wisely, but identify someone who will help you put your negative thoughts into perspective and restore a sense of confidence and calm.

The way another person perceives your speech can open doors or close them, build relationships or diminish them.

Four Phases

When researchers describe the arousal patterns for public speakers, they identify four conventional phases: *anticipation, confrontation, adaptation,* and *release*. Even if you don't speak in public, you've experienced these phases because they also occur in other high-stakes conversations such as interviews, important meetings, or difficult talks with people.

Peak anxiety usually occurs in the anticipation phase. Anticipation can trigger a core fear of uncertainty. When you don't know what is going to happen, you can allow your active imagination to take charge and visualize all sorts of unsettling scenarios.

While anxiety may persist through all four phases, it tends to decrease as you engage in the conversation or presentation. At that point, your mind is actively engaged in the task at hand, making it harder to simultaneously imagine unlikely scenarios. Also, as you communicate you become more comfortable, adapting to the reality as opposed to imagining something that is unlikely to happen. While all phases are important to manage, managing the phase that produces peak anxiety—anticipation—offers the greatest opportunity for lowering the type of stress that impacts your voice.[3]

In the anticipation phase, it is also not uncommon to catastrophize. Catastrophizing is when you imagine worst-case, irrational scenarios of what is about to happen. The key word here is *irrational.* It isn't just that you fear not answering the questions as well as you wanted or not getting the job. Those are logical fears. I'm talking about the scary, anxiety-producing movie that plays out in your head and spirals quickly into unlikely catastrophe. You picture the interview going so badly the hiring manager looks at your resumé, laughs in your face, and yells, "What made you think you were even *close* to qualified for this job?" Unlikely.

A friend of mine illustrated this as she told me how she catastrophized in college before an interview for a much-needed job. Here are the catastrophizing thoughts that plagued her before she went in:

> The interviewer started asking questions. I opened my mouth to answer, but nothing. Nothing would come out! My mind went completely blank. And then even when I tried to say something coherent, I was still too paralyzed to get it out. My thoughts began to turn on me. *Clearly, I'm incompetent*, I thought. *I am going to fail this interview. I'm not going to get the job. But I need the job or else I won't be able to pay my rent. I'm going get kicked out of my apartment. Why did I sign that lease for an apartment off campus? With nowhere to live, my grades are going to drop. And when that happens, I'm going to lose my scholarship! I can't lose my scholarship. I won't be able to pay tuition! I'm going to get kicked out of school! And that's not the worst of it. My parents already made it clear that after high school graduation, I can't live at home unless I'm in school. So soon I'm going to be a homeless college dropout with no place to go!*

Now, imagine these are the last thoughts you have before walking into a job interview. Will your vocal essence express the thoughts and emotions you most want to get across? Probably not.

In this scenario, my friend noticed her thoughts and decided she needed to calm herself and her thoughts just before the interview. She called a supportive friend who reminded her of how hardworking and friendly she is, two qualities important for the job. And she spent the last few minutes before the interview in the car taking deep breaths, praying, and envisioning herself speaking with ease and grace.

It worked. She says she stumbled a little in the interview, but her enthusiasm and authenticity overshadowed the stumbles. In fact, at one point when she didn't have a fast answer to a question, she said honestly, "I'm a little nervous."

She got the job. She never missed rent. Her grades didn't slip. She kept her scholarship. She stayed in school. And she never needed to beg her parents to reverse their stance on her living at home without being in school.

If you are aware, you can actually articulate what is happening when it is happening and take small actions that will alleviate your anxious thoughts, thereby calming the physiological responses that can feel out of your control.

Own your statements.

Improve the Sound of Your Voice

A person with a strong voice that is enjoyable to hear has an advantage over the person with a voice that is weak. A strong voice gets interrupted less often and commands more attention.[4] In professional settings, women tend to speak less, get interrupted more often, and have their statements analyzed more harshly. Interruptions are directly correlated with the strength of the speaker. If you have a strong voice, you are seen as more competent. These differences are significant when you have a message to deliver, want to be taken seriously, or need to influence a decision—whether in a personal setting or a professional one. Just as we walk without giving it a second thought, we talk without thinking about how to do it. But thinking about how your voice works can raise your awareness about how to improve the sound of it.

According to the American Academy of Otolaryngology, three components make up voice production:

- **Your Power Source** (Lungs)

  The power of your voice comes from the air that you exhale.

The more deeply you breathe, the stronger your voice. The airstream created in the trachea upon exhaling makes sound as it travels over your vocal cords. A strong, consistent airstream empowers clear sounds.

- **Your Voice Box** (Vibration)

Your larynx, commonly called the voice box, is located at the top of your windpipe and has two folds (your vocal cords) that vibrate quickly, producing the sound of your voice when air passes between them.

- **Your Resonator** (Throat, nose, mouth, and sinuses)

The sound that comes out of your mouth is influenced by the shape of the resonator tract, made up of your throat, nose, and mouth. This shape is unique to you and creates your unique sound. It also explains why your voice sounds different when you are sick. Problems such as inflammation change the shape of your resonator tract, creating a different sound altogether.

In professional settings, women tend to speak less, get interrupted more often, and have their statements analyzed more harshly.

Here are some practical ways to improve your own vocal essence.

1. **Breathe correctly.** To breathe correctly is to breathe from your diaphragm. Inhale through your nose and feel or watch your belly rise rather than your chest. When you inhale, your diaphragm tightens and moves downward. This increases the space in your chest cavity, allowing your lungs to expand. When you exhale, your diaphragm relaxes and moves upward, pushing air and carbon dioxide through the chest and out through your nose or mouth. This type of breathing literally gives you more life. It energizes you, relaxes you,

sharpens your mental state, and calms your emotions. Not only that, it supports a stronger sound when you speak.

2. **Stand up straight.** Poor posture constricts your breathing and weakens the airflow that will support your voice's power source. When you speak, make sure you sit or stand up straight, open your chest, and lift your head.

3. **Lower your pitch.** You may have heard or been told that to sound more confident, you should lower your voice. Interestingly, a British study cited in the *Daily Mail* points out that "a comparison of women's voices between 1945 and 1993 reveals they deepened significantly in the second half of the century. During that time, the average pitch of women aged 18 to 25 lowered by 23 hertz—equivalent to a semitone drop."[5]

   It is important to find the pitch that is authentic for you, however. Some of us have naturally higher-pitched voices, and that is just fine. What you don't want is a voice that has an artificially higher pitch as a result of insecurity or a lack of confidence. When you are not relaxed and don't inhale enough air to support your authentic voice, your voice sounds higher. When you don't feel strong, when deep down you want to send the subconscious message that you are helpless or childlike, you may speak in a voice that sounds more childlike. Of course, some women have medical conditions that create higher pitches, but that is not what we are talking about. The more grounded and rooted you are in speaking with truth and authenticity, the more grounded and rooted your voice will sound.

4. **Slow down.** Ever notice how much more quickly you speak when your emotions are running high—whether excited or nervous or upset? When your thoughts come rapidly, it is hard not to say them all at once in a rush. But when you speak quickly, others have to work too hard to grasp your message!

itisliketryingtoreadthesewordswithnospacebetweenthem! The substance of your message gets lost.

Talking too fast is also perceived as a sign of anxiety and lack of confidence. When you try hard to say things quickly, the subconscious message is that your words aren't all that important or that you believe people don't want to listen to you. If that's the case, people will certainly be more likely to pick up on that subconscious message and tune out. When you speak slowly and deliberately, it alerts them: "Listen up. This is important!" You and your message are both worthy of being heard, so deliver that message with care and intention.

You've probably noticed that most people don't listen well. This is critically important for you to remember because the most successful people take this fact into account. You want to make listening to you as easy as possible. If you speak too fast, your message will be missed. People may even tune out or catch just a couple of your points, and they may not even be the points you most wanted to make.

Don't make listening to you a chore. Make it easy. One of the quickest ways to do that is to deliberately slow the pace of your speech if you talk fast. Not too slow, though. Just as you don't want to lose them because you're talking too fast, you don't want to lose them because they're thinking, "Speed it up, will you!" Think of your favorite news anchor. That's generally a good pace. Clear and steady.

5. **Pay attention to your diction.** I was born in the South—North Florida, to be exact. My family is from South Carolina, and I spent many summers there as a child surrounded by grandparents, aunts and uncles, cousins, and friends we insist are somehow related if you dig back far enough in the family tree. Southern accents are like comfort food to me. I was always fixin' to do somethin'. Grandmama was always goin' o'er yonder to get somethin' outta the garden. And if you told him a big story about something that

sounded almost unbelievable, Grandaddy always responded, "Greeeaat day in the mornin'!" (Don't ask me why!) So just know that when I share this tip, it is with love and affection for a pattern of speech that loves to drop the last letter or two from the end of a word.

My southern accent morphed after moving to Denver in the fifth grade. I don't think people from Colorado have an accent of any sort. All of my adult life, people have enjoyed guessing where I'm from, but not one person has ever guessed right. Perhaps it is my penchant for fully pronouncing my words that throws them off! Anyway, remember this: When you drop important vowels and consonants, the people listening to you can miss the meaning of what you're saying. But they often won't tell you that. They'll fill in the blank themselves or they'll tune out. Either way, you've lost their attention.

Speaking too quickly, as discussed above, not only makes it hard for people to stay tuned in to your message but also impacts your diction. When you speak quickly, you don't breathe in enough air to support a strong-sounding voice. You may find that your mouth can't keep up with your mind. As a result, the endings of your words are weaker and less clear.

If you need extra help with your diction, consider taking singing or acting lessons to learn techniques for breathing, pronunciation, and projecting your voice well. Or try this exercise:

Use your smartphone or other voice recorder to record yourself reading a paragraph of text out loud. Before you record, mark a vertical line approximately every five words—use the end of a natural phrase to decide where to place the mark. Inhale a full breath before speaking each set of words. Speak each word fully, and fully pronounce the last syllable of each word. When you get to the next mark, stop. Inhale into your diaphragm again. Speak the next set of words. The purpose of this exercise isn't so that you talk like this in real life, but to practice over-enunciating so that your conversational diction becomes clearer.

6. **Adjust your volume.** Years ago, I interviewed a woman with a skill set and experience that would have been helpful to my business. My office was in an executive suite where multiple businesses shared a receptionist, lobby, and conference rooms, and our individual offices were right next to each other. As I interviewed the candidate, the volume of her voice was so loud that it carried two or three offices down the hallway. At first I thought it was just her laugh but quickly realized it was how she talked. It was distracting. And she was completely oblivious to it. What stands out to me is that years later, I don't remember her name, just her voice.

   Be aware of the volume of your voice and its effect on the people around you. Make sure your volume is appropriate for the setting. When there are more people around, you may need to speak up. When discussing sensitive information or needing people to lean in and feel connected, lower your voice. Volume is a powerful tool if you use it intentionally.

7. **Record yourself.** One of the most accurate and practical ways to improve your vocal essence is to listen to yourself on a recording. As a teenager, this technique is how I taught myself to sing. I would sing a verse into a tape recorder and then play it back to myself. What sounded good, I kept doing. What sounded off, I changed. I repeated this process until I got it right. It was a few years before I took any voice lessons. Record, listen, improve, and then rerecord. You'll be surprised at how quickly you can make tweaks that create a measurable improvement in how confident, warm, or strong you sound just by listening to the sound of your own voice.

8. **Pay attention to your voice inflection.** The emphasis you place on certain words, the warmth with which you speak,

and the certainty or uncertainty with which you end your statements all show up in your inflection. This is why two people can say exactly the same thing but their statements have two different meanings entirely.

Subtle changes in emphasis and inflection can change the entire meaning of what you say. In the following statement, there could be a total of seven different meanings. Say this statement out loud seven times, each time emphasizing a different word: *I never said she took my purse.*

9. **Remember "warmth" is powerful.** *Warmth* is one of the characteristics of people who are successful—who inspire, lead, and are most trusted. And one of the ways your warmth shines through is in the power of your voice. So how can you sound warmer? One way is simply to smile. It doesn't have to be a huge grin. Even a slight upturn of the corners of your mouth will do. A 2008 study from Amy Drahota, a research fellow at the University of Portsmouth in Great Britain, says that you can hear a smile.[6] People who are emotionally astute can distinguish different types of smiles merely by the sound of your voice.

Empathy can also be heard through your voice and is essential for being able to connect authentically with others. Empathy can mean pausing and letting someone else's voice be heard at a moment when you could keep talking. Or it can mean expressing that you hear people through a simple groan or whisper indicating you feel something as a result of their experience.

When people are in difficult moments, they aren't always looking for commentary. What they really want is acknowledgment. Friends want this from their friends. Husbands want it from their wives and wives from their husbands. Children want it from their parents. And it is what the coworker who didn't mean to mess up wants from his colleagues. A warm voice is like a snuggly blanket fresh from the dryer on a chilly day. It is a soft spot to rest, a place you long to return to each time you face a cold, hard day.

"Sounding like a success" seems so basic. And that's because it is. It isn't that you cannot be successful if your voice isn't warm or you talk too fast or your diction isn't clear. Not at all. There are plenty of examples of people who overcame first impressions or whose audiences loved the fact that they were none of these things at all. But success comes more easily when you sound like a success—when you are easy to listen to, when you sound authentic, when your voice is one others want to follow because you sound confident and warm at the same time. Your voice is the organ of the soul. Make sure that organ is tuned to express the essence of who you really are.

Your Script for Success

- Breathe deeply and often before opening your mouth to speak.

- Put your shoulders back, lift your head up, and stand straight when you speak. Not only will you feel more confident, but air will flow better and support your strongest-sounding voice.

- Slow down! When your emotions are high, you speak faster, but this makes it harder for others to process what you are saying.

- If you are on the phone, especially in important conversations, consider standing up to maximize the energy and sound of your voice.

- When you want to sound warm, smile.

Every Woman Should Know

- People are generally lazy listeners. An attractive-sounding voice commands attention, gets interrupted less often, and influences behavior and decisions.

- Your voice is powered by your breath. Practice breathing correctly and you'll lower anxiety, sound more confident, and usher in your most authentic voice.

- Upspeak is a fairly modern phenomenon that makes your statements sound like questions, causing people to doubt your certainty about what you're saying.

Coach Yourself

- What aspect of this chapter most resonates with you? What step do you feel led to take as a result?

- Notice how your voice changes when you feel insecure or threatened. Does it get higher? Become aggressive? Quiet? What actions could you take to restore your most authentic and confident voice when you feel insecure?

- Record yourself talking and listen for the following: 1) speaking from your diaphragm, 2) voice inflection and upspeak, 3) warmth, 4) talking speed, and 5) diction. Which area(s) do you want to actively improve? What step will you take forward and when?

Speak Differently

The human voice is the organ of the soul. Be intentional about how you express your thoughts and emotions through the power of your voice.

What You Say Without Saying a Word

*Your body language doesn't just affect how
others see you. It affects how you see yourself.*

I speak two languages, Body and English.
MAE WEST

Key Lessons

- Your mind doesn't just affect your body. Science shows that your body also changes your mind.

- "Power posing" will improve hormone levels in the brain that make you more comfortable, confident, passionate, and authentic.

- Small tweaks in your posture and appearance can mean big changes in your love life, your career, and your bank account.

- Becoming more attractive is easier and less superficial than you think.

I want you do something for me right now. I want you to smile. Not a half-hearted smile. Not a closed-mouthed, Kermit the Frog smile. But a show-all-your-teeth, puff-up-your-cheeks, let-your-eyes-crinkle sort of smile. You doing it yet? Okay. Good. Hold that smile.

Now, while you're smiling, I want you to notice that feeling you have. You know that inexplicable little tingle of effervescence you feel? That's actually serotonin and endorphins—feel-good chemicals that stimulate a sense of positivity in the brain.[1] Whether you're legitimately happy or just fix your face to look like you are happy by choosing to smile big—this is called a "Duchenne smile"—the muscles that contract trigger the release of serotonin and endorphins. I just love the fact that we don't just smile because we are happy, but we actually feel happier when we smile. Even if you just put a pencil in your mouth or make a hard "Eeee" sound, you still trigger those feel-good hormones.

But let's delve a little deeper. One of the reasons positive emotion is powerful is because it impacts your likelihood for greater success and happiness. According to multiple studies,[2] positive emotion expands your ability to deal with adversity and stress. It broadens your scope of thinking, meaning that you make better decisions after experiencing a boost of positive emotion. You are also more likely to engage in healthy behaviors such as exercise. Those who experience more positive emotion over time are more likely to get promoted, obtain a raise, and find themselves in a strong, lasting marriage. Positive emotion is not just correlated with success. It *causes* success.[3]

While smiling all by itself isn't going to produce success, it can change how you feel, which in turn can affect what you choose to do.

Smiling triggers a reaction that produces positive emotion, which leads to better and more accurate decision-making and stronger resilience.

If making a decision to change the physical state of our face can produce chemicals in the brain that make us feel good emotionally, what else could we change about our physical state that might improve our mental and emotional state? As it turns out, there are other ways in which you can make simple physical shifts that trigger these same reactions. They can produce greater confidence, willingness to take risks, and optimism—all of which are predictors of success.

Can a small tweak in my body language change my mind?

Your Body Is Powerful: Use It to Influence Your Mind

I'm nearing the end of a workday and just have to get through one final stretch. I am beginning to doubt I'll complete all the work I've set for myself in time. And I've been beating myself up for not getting focused earlier in the day. I am emphatic about leaving work at work so I can focus on my family, so I'm starting to feel a little stressed. I've been sitting, pondering a few concepts and ideas as I rest my elbow on the couple of inches of desktop space in front of my laptop. My head leans to the side, resting on my hand, which is gently holding the right side of my neck. Earlier, my head had rested on my right hand, which I had placed on my temple and forehead as I stared out the window.

Amy Cuddy, a social psychologist and professor at Harvard Business School, would call these positions "low-power poses." And as I noticed my low-power physical state, it occurred to me this would be a good time to intentionally engage in a "high-power pose."

I leaned back in my chair, hands clasped behind my head and elbows outstretched, ankles crossed and feet resting on my desk as I look out the window at the trees and pond that are the wooded, peaceful view outside my office. This is not something I've ever done before—perching my feet on my desk. Valid or not, such body language has seemed a bit cocky and masculine for my style. Besides, I wear a lot of skirts and dresses. Sometimes people walk past my office window. So it isn't practical. But sitting with your feet on a desk or table and leaning back with your elbows outstretched is a classic high-power posture, especially on television and in the movies. It's expansive body language that says, "I'm powerful."

I stayed in the position for two minutes. It was a simple tweak, and I noticed a subtle shift in my thoughts. With my arms open, I thought about the big picture of the work I am doing. I thought of my vision for the work. I reminded myself of past successes. The shift in thought wasn't huge. It was a perspective shift. You wouldn't have been able to see it while looking at me, but I felt it. It was subtle, but when I put my feet back on the ground and my hands back on the keyboard, I felt determined to reach my own personal finish line for the day before my husband and son picked me up to head home. And I did.

Professor Cuddy suggests we all try "power posing." In her book *Presence*, Cuddy researched the answer to an intriguing question:

> We know our minds change our bodies, but do our bodies also change our minds?[4]

The answer, as I found out when I changed my position, is yes. We tend to believe that our minds determine how we feel—both emotionally and physically. That is true. Becoming aware of your thoughts and intentionally choosing which ones to keep and which ones to replace is at the core of success and resilience.

But the reverse is not something we often think about, and it is true as well. What we do with our bodies can determine the thoughts that flow into our minds and the emotions we feel in our hearts. In other words, our body language causes specific reactions in the brain that impact our thoughts and emotions. It doesn't just happen when we flash a Duchenne smile. It happens when we position our body in certain ways and even move in certain ways.

Understanding the power of your body language is about much more than controlling your image and how other people feel about you. It is also about controlling how you feel about you and what you think. What you think is what you become. Proverbs 23:7 tells us, "As [a man] thinks in his heart, so is he" (NKJV).

So let's dive in a little deeper into the language you speak without saying a word. First, we will talk about how your body affects your mind, which ultimately shapes the actions you take that lead to success. Second, we'll talk about how your body language speaks volumes to the people around you and what you can do better to build meaningful connections, project confidence and credibility, and invite more love and authenticity into your life.

If making a decision to change the physical state of our face can produce chemicals in the brain that make us feel good emotionally, what else could we change about our physical state that might improve our mental and emotional state?

How to Position Your Body for More Confidence

All of us want to feel powerful. In your most powerful state, you are comfortable in your own skin. You are passionate and purposeful. You are enthusiastic and authentic. You tell the truth and act with courage. So when I talk about being powerful, I am talking about the moments

High-Power Poses

- Reclined in a seat with your feet up on a table, hands clasped behind your head and elbows outstretched
- Standing with your feet shoulder-width apart, hands on your hips and elbows out
- Standing with your feet shoulder-width apart and both hands stretched at a 45-degree angle over your head

Low-Power Poses:

- Standing with your feet together and your arms crossed or hands loosely hugging your body
- Sitting with your shoulders hunched and arms close to the body
- Sitting with your head down and arms cradled

From a physiological standpoint, what these "poses" represent is your becoming either bigger or smaller. Taking up more space with outstretched arms, legs, or feet symbolizes a more powerful stance. And it signals to the brain a more powerful feeling, leading to the likelihood of more powerful attitudes and actions. Lowering your head, slumping your shoulders, and bringing your feet together and your limbs closer to your body symbolizes retreat, hiding, self-protection, and smallness. And such body language signals to the brain a less powerful feeling, making powerless attitudes and actions more likely.

in which you show up in your life exactly as God intended you to be—standing in truth, light, and love. In this state, you don't need to hide. You don't make excuses. You make the most of "what is." You see possibilities and have the faith to believe they can come to fruition—and you act on that faith. You push through challenges. You allow yourself to feel what you feel, but you don't allow the emotions to control you.

You are your most powerful when you're not worried about fulfilling the expectations of others but about fulfilling the purpose and assignments for which you were created. A woman of faith might say it this way: You are most powerful when you stop worrying about impressing others and keep your focus on impressing God. In that powerful place, you find your most authentic self. You connect with the essence of success—a harmony of purpose, resilience, and joy. You experience love, perseverance, faith, meaning, and positive relationships. And believe it or not, your body language can correlate with all of these.

Here's what happens when you feel powerful. In one study, Cuddy and her colleagues measured the testosterone and cortisol levels of study participants by testing their saliva. Then they had one group of participants hold high-power poses for two minutes while the other group held low-power poses for two minutes. After the two minutes were up, they gave the participants the option of engaging in a high-risk game.

Following the game, they tested saliva samples a second time to compare the before and after testosterone and cortisol levels. Testosterone is correlated with being more optimistic, confident, and willing to take risks—all of which are traits of powerful people. The most successful women have all three of these traits. Cortisol, on the other hand, is released in reaction to stress. Low cortisol levels in the face of a challenge indicate a calmer or more laid-back response to stress. This also is a trait of powerful people. It isn't that they avoid stressful situations or challenges. It is that they are able to maintain a sense of control and calm under pressure.

Here's what happened in the study. Those who held high-power poses for two minutes saw a 20 percent increase in testosterone levels and a 25 percent decrease in cortisol levels. Those who held low-power poses saw a 10 percent decrease in testosterone levels and a 15 percent increase in cortisol levels. Additionally, 86 percent of the high-power group opted for the high-risk game while only 60 percent of the low-power group wanted to play the game. Two minutes can change your brain and create feelings that lead to entirely different behavior.

Keep in mind, these "poses" are specifically about influencing how you feel, not how others feel. At your next work meeting, I don't suggest throwing your feet up on the table and leaning back with your arms behind your head so that everyone in the meeting can "feel" your confidence. However, if you are about to go into a meeting and are feeling anxious or doubtful about being effective in what you need to communicate, take a couple of minutes alone to power pose. If you are headed into an interview or important conversation and you're sitting and waiting for the other person, don't sit hunched over your cell phone scrolling through the latest social media posts. Instead, throw your shoulders back, lift your head, and take up space.

Those who held high-power poses for two minutes saw a 20 percent increase in testosterone levels and a 25 percent decrease in cortisol levels.

High- and Low-Power Poses

Here's a more complete rundown of a few high-power poses to try and low-power poses to avoid when you want to shift your mind toward feeling more powerful and less powerless. I've included their names to help you more easily remember them:

The Superhero

There's a good reason Wonder Woman stands the way she does! Legs shoulder-width apart, both hands placed firmly on hips, shoulders and hips squared off and facing forward. It turns out positioning your body in this way boosts feelings of confidence, optimism, and willingness to take risks.

The Bear Stance

I like to call this pose the "bear stance" because I can picture a bear on his hind legs with his paws up. Stand with your feet shoulder-width apart and put your hands out to form a "V" above your shoulders.

The Executive

The "executive" is the pose I held at my desk. Lean back, clasp your hands behind your head, and rest your feet on a table or desk with your ankles crossed.

The Pity Party

Sit with your shoulders slumped, your elbow on the table or in your lap, and forehead in your hand—or worse yet, forehead in both hands. The pity party is the body language of defeat.

The Cold Mama

This low-power pose reminds me of how my mom looks—all moms perhaps—when she's chilly: arms wrapped around the upper body, limbs as close to the body as possible, and head down. You can almost see her sliding her hands up and down over her arms to warm herself.

The Shrunk-a-Hunch

Just look around. You'll see people everywhere shrinking and hunching over. It seems more common than ever because so many are tied to their smartphones, tablets, and laptops. I call that body language the "shrunk-a-hunch." When you do it, your body language is all about becoming smaller. In some cases, you might even want to feel invisible.

Your shoulders cave inward, your arms and hands fold in front of you or stay very close to the body, and your head is down. This body positioning can occur whether you are sitting or standing. I like to think of it as the "texting" position. And even when you're standing, you are still not upright. The woman who does the shrunk-a-hunch appears smaller than she actually is—and she feels smaller too.

Interestingly, not only do these stances trigger specific hormones in the brain and cause you to feel more confident or less confident, but these poses also speak a message to anyone who sees you. There are, of course, many other ways to position your body, but keep in mind that the body positions that empower you to feel most powerful and authentic are positions that are open, tall, and welcoming.

What You Say Without Saying a Word

As Barbara sat across from Pamela pouring out her heart and hoping for some answers, Pamela did something she often did when she was about to share something profound. Barbara had caught onto it recently during their counseling sessions. Pamela, a licensed therapist with a track record of helping clients have major breakthroughs and muster the courage to make big shifts in their lives, would make a distinctive gesture with her hands. She'd clasp her hands with her pointing fingers touching. Her thumbs side by side under her chin and those pointing fingers placed vertically just over her lips and nose, her eyes would narrow and her breathing would become audible—almost as though she were breathing in Barbara's words more deeply to better process all that she was saying.

Barbara didn't quite understand why, but whenever Pamela did this, Barbara felt a deep wave of support rush over her. She knew Pamela was fully present, immersed in the issues that were so deeply personal, and contemplating how best to support Barbara's goals and well-being. "I can't explain it," Barbara told me. "But those moments are the moments I felt like a breakthrough was about to happen. And it always was."

Barbara's feelings and instincts about Pamela were right. In fact, the body language Pamela displayed during those counseling sessions is a variation of a something called "steepling." Fingertips to fingertips often communicates authority. Whether the pointed steeple as described by Barbara, a full steeple in which all five fingertips on one hand touch all five fingertips on the other hand, or a modified steeple in which it looks like you are holding a basketball, all have the effect of conveying thoughtfulness, authority, and compassion. Pamela's body language triggered a response in Barbara that led her to feel she was in a "safe space" and in competent hands. As a result, she opened up more fully, with the hope that she'd get the help and answers she needed. That helped Pamela better succeed in her role as Barbara's counselor.

Seemingly small shifts in body language can
create big shifts in the flow of communication.

We've already discussed how your body language affects how you feel about yourself and shapes your thoughts, which lead to your actions. Now let's take a look at how your body language shapes how others feel about you.

First, while there are many generalities that can hold true, there is no one-size-fits all explanation of body language. For example, it is widely suggested that crossing your arms means you are closed off from other people. Sometimes that is true. Sometimes the opposite is true. It could also mean you are tired. Or you are settling into a conversation and getting comfortable. Or it might mean you are closed off, tired, interested in the conversation, and want to get comfortable all at the same time! My point? Don't be too quick to definitively declare the meaning of someone else's body language. People who know you are better able to read your body language than perfect strangers.

Body language communicates emotional intent. In other words, what you feel. Research shows that whatever you are feeling, your body communicates that feeling even before your conscious mind processes it. The time delay is extremely quick, less than one second, but it is real. Whether you're happy or irritable, tired or hungry, your body will signal those feelings first. Your face will also convey those feelings.

Most adults are very good at manipulating their facial expressions to disguise any feelings that would be counterproductive to their goals in the present moment. We are less likely, though, to be conscious of what our bodies are communicating.

Some general guidelines can help *you* speak the right body language to maximize your chances of connecting in a powerful way with others, influencing decisions and ideas, and boosting your confidence so that you take the next step—especially when it requires courage in the face of doubt, insecurities, and fear.

Body positions that empower you to feel most powerful and authentic are positions that are open, tall, and welcoming.

Take Up Space

If you want your body language to convey your confidence, know that such power is communicated nonverbally through the use of height and space. Those who are traditionally in power tend to feel like they belong in the spaces and positions of power in which they find themselves. Those who are new to power or are denied power often feel they don't belong even when they know logically they do. As a result, those who feel powerless use body language that takes up less space. Their body language often consists of low-power poses, almost automatically. So when we consider that women have been less likely to hold such positions, we can revert to such habits.

The first rule of thumb for increasing your confidence, influence, and courage is to simply take up more space. What do I mean? Stand up straight. Stand tall. If you're five foot one like me, stand as if you are six foot one. If you are a six foot one woman, don't hide it! Don't shrink from your height. Own it.

Don't Be Afraid to Widen Your Stance

In line with taking up space, don't be afraid to widen your stance. Your feet do not have to be neatly pressed together while you're standing around having casual conversation. Standing with your feet too close together can make you appear hesitant and unsure of yourself. Set your feet a comfortable distance apart. Relax your lower body, including your knees. I'm not talking about two feet here, but a few inches is natural and projects a sense of being grounded and confident.

Smile

Remember what I said about a "Duchenne smile" releasing serotonin and endorphins to your brain, making you feel positive emotion? Well, smiling also has an effect on the people on the receiving end of your pearly-white grin. Duke University researchers discovered that we remember people who smile at us. Smiles activate the brain's reward centers, making it easier to recall the names of smilers. The brain interprets a genuine smile to mean you are warm and trustworthy.

Make Positive Eye Contact

Make it a point to notice the shape and color of a person's eyes when you meet them. That's one easy way to be present in the moment. Do they have deep-set eyes? Wide eyes? Long eyelashes? Curved brows? Notice something distinctive enough that you could describe something simply about their eyes. This should take only a few seconds, which is plenty of time to make positive eye contact.

Don't Fidget

When you feel uncomfortable or anxious, a natural response can be to fidget—twirling your hair, biting your nails, messing with your necklace, sucking on your lip. All of these are just self-soothing mechanisms. Fidgeting not only projects insecurity but causes the people around you to feel uncomfortable. It takes away from the message you are trying to communicate—whether to one person or in front of a group of people. Start catching yourself in the act and stop it. Take a deep breath, get still, and plant yourself firmly with both feet on the floor. Notice any low-power body language and shift to high-power body language immediately—shoulders back, arms open, head up. Now, relax.

Make Gestures of Agreement

People love to be affirmed. And one of the ways you can do that through body language is to find points of agreement and gesture in the affirmative. The most common gesture of agreement is a simple nod. A pat on the back or a squeeze on the arm when someone shares good news is another gesture of agreement.

Of course, make sure not to use gestures that include touch unless it's appropriate for that relationship. Be wise and use your discernment. In opposite-sex professional relationships, it could be misconstrued. If you don't know the person well, be respectful of their space. But in relationships in which there is an established trust and affection, respectful touch communicates warmth.

Don't Tilt Your Head

Instinct tells us that a head tilt, which exposes the neck, signals vulnerability and surrender. In fact, people who scrunch their shoulders upward symbolically are trying to protect themselves from perceived danger in their environment. So generally speaking, tilting your head, especially when sharing valuable or important information, sends mixed signals. It communicates that you are unsure and not confident about what you're saying. Keep that in mind during conversations where the credibility of what you are sharing is important. In casual conversations, head tilting is not problematic.

Get Your Handshake Right

You've probably heard it before, but it is always worth a reminder. A firm but not too firm (no death grip!) handshake speaks volumes. Practice it. Use it. Always make positive eye contact when you shake hands, long enough to remember the color or shape of the person's eyes. To convey warmth or gratitude, place your left hand over the shaking hands as you say "hello" or "thank you."

Walk Down Memory Lane

If there is one thing that can boost your confidence and body language quickly, it is remembering your own testimony. Think back to a time when you were anxious or afraid of fumbling a conversation, presentation, or other opportunity, but you didn't. Instead, you did great. You succeeded. In fact, you forgot you were ever nervous about it in the first place.

Go back to the place to boost your faith to believe in the possibility of succeeding in this next test. Recalling your past faith-filled moments will alleviate your anxiety and give you the courage to step forward with confidence.

Appearance Is a Language of Its Own

When I was 22, I landed my first full-time job. My title was "marketing secretary," but my long-term vision was an opportunity to lead and eventually start my own business in public relations. It was my first job, and I was enamored with the idea of being in the professional world. I shopped for a professional work wardrobe that reflected the people whose positions were similar to what I aspired to. That basically meant stylish but appropriate dresses and suits.

On a couple of occasions, I was asked by coworkers why I was "dressed up." Knowing that not everyone has earned the right to be privy to my vision, I always answered that I enjoyed wearing dresses and skirts.

My opportunity came more quickly than I ever expected. Within about three months, my boss left, and the company began the search for a marketing director to replace her. I worked hard to share my ideas and keep things running smoothly. And within just a few weeks of my boss's departure, I was offered a six-month trial promotion as the new marketing director.

I was not qualified on paper for the job. But I worked hard and had a solid education. And one of my functions in the position was representing the company from a marketing perspective. If I had not dressed for where I was going, I am not sure the decision makers—some of whom were 30 and 40 years my senior—would have been able to imagine me in the position. My attention to my appearance was one of many clues they used to decide whether to take a risk on a very young woman for that position. Of course, a positive appearance wasn't the reason for granting me the opportunity. However, a poor appearance would definitely have been a reason for them to withhold it.

Appearance is a language of its own. And like any other language, you must learn to speak it well in order to communicate successfully. We all like to say, "Don't judge a book by its cover," but it's a futile statement because we all do. In fact, we are biologically wired to do so. It is self-preservation. Our brains are always on the lookout for cues. Is this person trustworthy? Are they credible? Are they out to get me? Should I spend the finite amount of time I have on my calendar with them?

Should I invest my resources here? To answer those questions, we must begin somewhere. And the easiest place to start is with what we see.

As much as we'd like to believe that looks don't matter, they do. Putting effort into your appearance yields results that influence people's decisions about you. I'm not placing a judgment on the political correctness of this. It seems life would be fairer if it were not true. Appearance can build your credibility or dismantle it. Remember, this is why it is important to consider how successful women "speak differently." We speak not just through our words but through everything we project into the world—and that includes appearance.

A 2005 study by researchers at the University of Pennsylvania's Cognitive Neuroscience Center found that those who are physically more attractive reap a lot of unearned rewards for their looks—from higher wages to more romantic choices. The interesting caveat is that the judgment on attractiveness happens so rapidly, in less than a second, yet impacts major decisions about how the perceiver is influenced by what he sees. Looks are difficult for humans to ignore. Therefore, it is difficult to deny their importance in social evaluations.

Study after study confirms that appearance matters—not just for women, but for men too. In fact, those considered more attractive benefit from a "halo effect." A halo effect happens when you have one positive characteristic that is so powerful it overshadows other attributes and impacts how others see you. In studies, people rate attractive people as kinder, smarter, and more trustworthy than people they consider unattractive. There is a partiality, however shallow it may be, that allows attractive people to obtain help more readily and to sway the opinions of others. So what does this mean for you?

It means that your appearance will impact your influence. This is not to say there is one particular way to be or look attractive. Attractiveness is subjective. But making the most of your inner and outer beauty is definitely a form of speaking differently. Keep in mind that what's attractive to one person may not be attractive at all to another. Consider the person(s) you most want to influence when deciding what your best choices are. The teacher who dresses a little bit quirky might be viewed differently by administrators than her students, but if her primary goal is to influence and connect with her students, her choices might be just perfect for her goal. When trying to influence others, consider whether your appearance builds a bridge to your goal or a detour from it.

A good friend of mine in the fashion industry has an assistant I'll call Shelly. Shelly is super capable and, according to my friend, she is one of the hardest-working people she has ever seen. Plus she's humble and exceedingly helpful. "When I show up to work at a shoot, Shelly is always two steps ahead of me," she explains. "I can totally relax and focus on the work at hand."

There is one thing, however, that she'd like to see Shelly do differently. "We are constantly in environments where Shelly could make contacts that would open much bigger doors for her. But I can see that no one takes her seriously. She isn't thoughtful about the way she dresses or her hair or makeup. This is the fashion industry. If it matters in any profession, it matters in mine! I've said this to her several times, but she blows off the advice and starts talking about how hard she works and what she knows. The thing is, no one is going to be interested in what she *knows* if her appearance doesn't communicate the message that she *cares*—that she's willing to go the extra mile."

Appearance is a language of its own.

It is easy to dismiss the subject of appearance as superficial. But my friend makes a profound point. When you take time to intentionally look your best, you broadcast something very specific about yourself—attention to detail, a willingness to "go the extra mile." The message you send is that you care. Whether you look "put together" or a complete and utter mess, your appearance speaks volumes about who you are before you even have a chance to open your mouth. This applies in your personal life as much as your professional life. It isn't so much about what style you choose, but that you choose to look intentional in a way that reflects your uniqueness, personal preferences, and values.

I am reminded of the power of personal appearance to tell a story when I think of my mother-in-love. She passed away just six days after my husband and I became engaged. Besides blessing me immensely by her sheer joy at the love her son and I share, I was always struck by the meticulous care she took in her appearance. It would have been noteworthy for the average healthy woman. But Miss Dolores, as I called her, was very ill. I never saw her walk because she used a wheelchair. She was often tired and had to retire to her room to rest. But when she came out, she was always dressed in something lovely. Her nails were groomed and she wore lipstick, earrings, and a warm, welcoming smile every single time I visited. Her eyes danced with anticipation when we chatted. The power of her presence was enhanced by the care in her appearance.

I wish I had known her longer, but it made such an impression on me that she insisted on presenting herself with such dignity and grace even until the end. This is something about which I will always remind her grandchildren. Her appearance told a story. She was a talented artist, and her work hangs on the walls in our home. And she loved fashion. There was never a day I saw her that she didn't compliment something I was wearing. Even when I visited her in the hospital, she noticed my hair, my jewelry, my outfit! She appreciated beauty and excellence in all things visual. And her personal appearance told that story about her personality.

What story does your appearance tell about you? Since we are talking about how successful women speak differently, it is a reasonable question to ask: "What exactly does your appearance 'speak' of you?"

This isn't about being pretty or not pretty, gorgeous or not. It is about being "attractive." Attractive is an overall appearance that is pleasant to the eye. And the things that make you more attractive are within your control. The goal is to make the most of your God-given looks by being thoughtful about your appearance.

Some of the research about attractiveness is unsettling, but it points to the impact of visual communication on your ability to influence others and reach your goals. Particularly when the goals are financial, it seems physical appearance has an illogical but undeniable impact. For example, tall people get paid more—nearly $800 per year for every inch of height, according to researchers at the University of Florida. So someone six inches taller who has comparable skills will average $5000 more per year in annual income. (I don't recommend wearing heels to try to make up for the height. I tried that in my twenties, and I'm still paying the price.)

Unfortunately, the advantages don't stop at height. Those who have a Body Mass Index (BMI) above 30 are also paid less—almost $9000 per year less for women and close to $5000 per year less for men, according to a study at George Washington University.[5] A BMI over 30 is classified as obese. Exercise also appears to impact income—those who work out regularly make about 9 percent more than those who don't. And like it or not, women who wear makeup are rated as more confident and earn up to 30 percent more than their non-makeup-wearing peers.[6] The makeup must be worn in moderation, however. Too much makeup has the opposite effect.[7] Appearance affects your income if you are employed. In social situations, it impacts whose attention you attract or don't attract.

Your appearance is a form of communication. So ask yourself, "What does my appearance communicate to those around me—at work, in social settings, at church, and in my community? Is that the message I want to communicate, or is it time for some tweaks and changes?"

Take a look in the mirror and be honest with yourself. Do you need to pay closer attention to your personal grooming?

The changeable actions you can take that have the greatest impact include:

- **Countenance:** Your attitude shows on your face, in the way you walk, and in whether or not you smile. The human brain will notice a smile from up to 300 feet away. It is as if the brain scans the environment looking for a smile.

- **Posture:** We've talked a lot about high-power and low-power poses, but at the most basic level, improving your posture makes you immediately more attractive. If you have poor posture, make it a goal to improve your posture every day. Set a reminder on your phone or strategically place sticky notes in places to remind yourself to hold your head up and stand up straight.

- **Wardrobe:** As a general rule, remember this: Don't dress for where you are in life right now. Dress for where you are going. A few years ago, I took a flight from Atlanta to New York in the month of October. It was 80 degrees in Atlanta and had been in that temperature range since the spring. I forgot that it might not feel like summer up north. I arrived with short sleeves and no coat. As I was walking out of the airport, a blast of cold air shocked me into reality. "Oh, my goodness," I said to the driver as the 40-degree air hit my bare arms. "I didn't even bring a coat." He looked at me with such utter disbelief, I don't think I'll ever forget his expression. "It's October," he said as though I didn't realize what month we were in. "This is New York." Ask yourself this question: If you were already living the life to which you aspire, what would you look like? What would you wear? Speak life into your vision by dressing for the vision.

- **Grooming:** Being clean, neat, and fresh is the foundation of a positive appearance. When any of these elements is missing, it can leave such a stain on the impression you make that you may never overcome it. Pay especially close attention to things such as your hair and skin. Style your hair intentionally: Get it cut, keep it healthy. Make sure your nails are neat. This isn't about whether you wear nail polish or faux nails or nail wraps or nothing at all, but about whether they look intentionally cared for. Take care of your skin and keep it moisturized. There's nothing like shaking hands with someone with dry, cracked hands or glancing down at someone's open-toed shoes only to see unkempt feet. What does that communicate about the person? Maintain your teeth. Get them cleaned twice a year, do what your dentist says, and have fresh breath. Plenty of well-qualified people lose great opportunities because of issues as fixable as bad breath or sad-looking hair. But they never realize it because no one wanted to insult them by telling them. Take a look in the mirror and be honest with yourself. Do you need to pay closer attention to your personal grooming?

The Myth of Attractiveness

There is a Scripture I just love in which Samuel is talking to Saul and puts things into perspective. He says, "For man looks at the outward appearance, but the Lord looks at the heart" (1 Samuel 16:7 NKJV). More than anything else that can impact your outward appearance, your attitude, compassion and a spirit of service will all shine through. In fact, your inner beauty will literally change people's perceptions of your outer beauty. The gleam in your eye that comes from loving what you do every day; the smile on your face that emerges from your gratitude, faith and love; and the strength in posture that is transformed by confidence—all of these embody the spirit that is seen all over you. The myth of a women's attractiveness is that it is about "prettiness." But that isn't it. Attractiveness is appeal. It is how much you attract others to want to be around you and influenced by you.

Your Script for Success

- When prepping for an important conversation or event, try "power posing" to boost hormones that increase confidence and optimism and lower your stress level.

- Avoid low-power poses in your everyday posture. Become aware when you do these and immediately shift your position to feel more powerful.

- Be intentional about your appearance. Take an honest look at yourself. Even have a trusted friend or adviser give you feedback. Make changes that allow you to express the essence of who you are through your appearance.

Every Woman Should Know

- The positioning of your body can literally change the hormonal makeup of your body chemistry in the moment, causing you to feel more or less confident.

- Your smile can be seen from up to 300 feet away and changes how people see you and feel about you.

- Appearance is a language of its own that triggers automatic responses in people. It can work to your advantage or disadvantage, depending on the care and attention you give it.

Coach Yourself

- What aspect of this chapter most resonates with you? What step do you feel led to take as a result?

- What activity is coming up in the next 24 to 48 hours for which you want a boost of confidence? For two minutes, before you begin interaction with others for that activity, hold one of the power poses—the Executive, the Superhero, or the Bear Stance—for two full minutes. After the event, meeting, or activity, reflect on your level of confidence, optimism, and risk taking.

- What aspect of your appearance makes you feel most confident? Why? What aspect of your appearance causes you to feel insecure or self-critical? What could you do that would empower you to enhance it, embrace it, and celebrate it?

Speak Differently

Your body language and appearance are powerful forms of communication. Be intentional about speaking the right language to move your vision forward.

Learn to Flip the Script

*Responding in ways that are unexpected can
yield results that border on miraculous.*

*To win against your enemies you have to do the
opposite of what they expect you to do.*
SONYA PARKER

Key Lessons

- Sometimes your most powerful weapon in contentious conversations is compassion.

- Non-complementary behavior, doing the opposite of what's expected, can create breakthroughs.

- Setting clear boundaries in relationships will yield you results where other people could not seem to make headway.

The intriguing NPR program *Invisibilia* shared a remarkable story that defies common logic. It left me speechless and is a brilliant illustration of the powerful effect of counterintuitive reactions in contentious situations.

On a warm summer evening in Washington, DC, a group of eight friends was celebrating life and recent milestones over hors d'oeuvres at a backyard dinner party. "It was like a magical night," as Michael, who attended with his wife and teenage daughter, described it. While standing next to his wife enjoying the evening, he suddenly saw a long-barrel handgun between them. A man had stealthily crashed the party, first pointing the gun at a friend and then turning it to Michael's wife—directly at her head. He demanded money and aggressively threatened to start shooting if they didn't comply.

Everyone stood in shock. Even worse, none of them had any cash on them. They began scrambling for what to say to defuse the situation. Even through his expletive-laced demands, Michael says the robber looked anxious and nervous. Maybe they could somehow say something to prevent this nightmare from becoming a tragedy. They decided to try guilt.

"We asked, 'What would your mother think of you?'" Michael recalled, hoping it would guilt the gunman into changing his mind.

Instead, it seemed to escalate his behavior. Things became tenser. He became more agitated as he yelled back, "I don't have a [expletive] mother!" Things seemed to be moving toward an end no one wanted.

That's when a friend at the table named Christina made an offer. It was counterintuitive and probably made out of sheer desperation.

"Look," she said calmly. "We are here celebrating. Why don't you have a glass of wine—and sit down."

Michael describes it as a "switch." "You could feel the difference," he recalled. "It was definitely the right thing to say."

Suddenly the man's face changed. They poured him a glass of wine. He tasted it and remarked how good it was. They offered him something to eat. He sat down. He put the gun in his pocket. And soon after, he murmured under his breath, "I think I've come to the wrong place."

They offered words of understanding. And in his reflection in the quietness and oddness of the situation, he made a request.

"He said something so strange," Michael explained. He asked for a hug. They all hugged him. Then he said, "I'm sorry," and walked out with a glass of wine in his hand.

Michael described the turn of events to NPR as a "miracle."

And it certainly was. There is also a psychological description for what happened. It is the idea that we tend to mirror behavior when interacting with others. When you are kind, other people are more likely to return the kindness. When you are rude, others are likely to return your rudeness with more of the same.

The unbelievable turnaround of that night at the dinner party reminds me of Ashley Smith, a young woman I interviewed years ago after she made national headlines deescalating a hostage situation by using Rick Warren's bestseller *The Purpose-Driven Life* to engage her kidnapper in a conversation about his life purpose. Her captor had stunned the nation when he escaped a courtroom where he was on trial for rape, murdered four people including a judge, and then forced his way into then-30-year-old Ashley's home, holding her hostage. It was his conversation with Ashley, in which she spoke to him about purpose and meaning, that ultimately led to a safe ending for her. He eventually turned himself in.[1]

Stand firm in who you are. Let your words reflect the essence of love instead of fear.

Hopefully, you won't have to deal with situations as serious as the one that group of friends experienced, but you might have to deal with a difficult personal relationship. The concept of complementarity[2] offers insight into how you can turn difficult everyday situations around through the power of your vocal essence—not just what you say, but how you say it and the warmth with which you say it. It offers a powerful tool to use when you need to abruptly halt the spiral of negativity.

The key to breaking the pattern is to refuse to return negative behavior with negative, which typically results in escalating the situation rather than deescalating it. To break the pattern, return negative behavior with the unexpected. Doing so is called non-complementary behavior. Once the pattern is broken, the other party—following the pattern of complementary behavior—then mirrors you. To be clear, this is not easy to do. But it can be very powerful.

From a faith perspective, this concept is aligned with the words of Jesus Himself as He astonished the Pharisees with such radical declarations as this:

You have heard that it was said, "Love your neighbor and hate your enemy." But I tell you, love your enemies and pray for those who persecute you, that you may be children of your Father in heaven. He causes his sun to rise on the evil and the good, and sends rain on the righteous and the unrighteous. If you love those who love you, what reward will you get? Are not even the tax collectors doing that? And if you greet only your own people, what are you doing more than others? Do not even pagans do that? (Matthew 5:43-47).

In other words, it says nothing of your faith to do what everyone else does. It speaks volumes about your faith when you are able to remain rooted in who you are—warm, kind, loving—even when other people are not those things. In fact, it is a test of your faith to be able to exemplify those values when others exemplify the opposite.

Stand firm in who you are. Let your words reflect the essence of love instead of fear.

One of my favorite Scriptures is 1 John 4:18, which states that "perfect love casts out fear" (NKJV). When people act in ugly ways, it is fear. When they are rude, it is fear. When they gossip, it is fear. And when we respond in kind, it is fear—our fear that maybe they are right, maybe they will get the upper hand, maybe we are not as powerful as we believe. But fear cannot cast out fear. Only love can.

Yvette Cook is CEO of Usher's New Look, a nonprofit founded in 1999 by eight-time Grammy winner Usher Raymond that has trained more than 30,000 underserved high school students in six major cities since that time. A full 100 percent of students who go through the four-year, research-based curriculum developed in conjunction with Emory University graduate from high school, even though the graduation rate in these students' schools hovers around 68 percent. And 98 percent of the students enroll in college upon high school graduation. Yvette is passionate about service. Her ability to communicate effectively in challenging situations has been a hallmark of her highly successful career path.

Yvette was a young, up-and-coming sales account executive when she was assigned to the most dreaded client at the entire television station where she worked. The day before the account was handed over to her, she stumbled on an account executive who had previously been assigned the client. The account executive was trying to pull herself together, having been brought to tears when the client cursed her out over some trivial matter. Now it was Yvette's turn.

"The buyer was a terror," Yvette explains. "She was literally in charge of millions of dollars in advertising for a major Fortune 500 company for over 15 years. And she was a bully." Not long after she took over the account, predictably, the client called Yvette upset about something. She was yelling into the phone and cursing, and Yvette was completely taken off guard. But her reaction was quite unconventional.

"I can't explain it, but I instinctively hung up the phone," she says of the incident. You read that right. In the middle of the yelling and cursing, she gently put the phone back down on the receiver.

"She called right back," Yvette remembers.

"What happened?" the client said.

"I hung up," Yvette replied honestly and in a neutral tone. "Once you calm down, why don't you call me back?"

Then something happened that had never happened in all of the years the station had been dealing with this client.

"She instantly calmed down," Yvette remembers. "And she never raised her voice at me again. She never cursed. She was always respectful."

To be clear, the client did not suddenly become respectful with everyone, but with Yvette, she behaved differently. Yvette flipped the script. She didn't react to the client's awful, unprofessional behavior with complementary behavior such as anger or crying or appeasing. She set a boundary. She would always communicate with her, but she would never tolerate being yelled and cursed at.

Yvette's approach goes deeper than that, though. Listen to what else she said about the client.

"She was prone to unusual and very wide mood swings, and I believed it was a mental health issue," she observed. "If her hair was down, she was doing great. She was fun to be around. If her hair was in a bun, she was the other woman."

Rather than taking it personally, Yvette stepped back to look at the situation from a broader view. She remained focused on the business of the relationship—selling advertising to the client and maintaining a workable relationship.

One of the most counterproductive habits of women who are not as successful is to take someone's bad behavior personally. Remember this: When someone behaves dysfunctionally, it isn't about you. It is about them. Don't allow it to change who you are when you interact with them. It will take a greater level of presence and strength to deal with them without being thrown off balance. Take a deep breath. Then *choose* your response instead of reacting impulsively. Yvette's client had treated every single account executive disrespectfully. Prior to Yvette, they had all endured her rants, cursing, and unreasonable demands. So it wasn't personal. It was universal. *She* was the problem.

Eventually, her problem ended her career. "One day," Yvette explained, "she threw a tape dispenser at a temp agency worker and she was fired." It is a sad story, really. And Yvette can look back on the situation with compassion and realize that this woman's emotional issues had cost her job and a handsome salary she had worked hard to attain. She had attained "success" by worldly standards, but not by the definition we use in this book. Success is a harmony of purpose, resilience, and joy. Successful women are compassionate. They are wise. They are kind. They speak up with courage but don't destroy others in the process.

Anxiety Reappraisal

Another great example of flipping the script is a technique called "anxiety reappraisal." The concept is simply that our words have power. They can reinforce counterproductive thoughts and emotions…or help undo them.

Let's take the counterproductive emotion that most of us feel at some point or another: anxiety. Say you're about to have an important conversation, such as a job interview or meeting your significant other's parents for the first time. You're thinking about how you might say the wrong thing. You worry you won't connect. You picture it going all wrong…and as you do, you feel worse. More nervousness ensues. And you are pulling up for the meeting. You've got five minutes. You tell yourself to relax or calm down. "Stay calm. Breathe."

But when you are really nervous, relaxing and calming down are pretty hard to do. The butterflies don't go away. The irrational thoughts don't suddenly disappear. Anxiety is a high arousal state. Your heart beats faster, your cortisol (stress) levels go up, and your body prepares to take action. Calm is the opposite, so it seems only natural that trying to calm down is the antidote to being anxious. But the better answer is counterintuitive.

Instead of telling yourself to relax, tell yourself you're "excited." Excitement, like anxiety, is a high arousal state, explains Alison Wood Brooks, a professor and researcher at Harvard. It is actually a much smaller leap to go from anxious to excited than to go from anxious to calm. So intentionally speak the word *excitement*. Own it.[3]

Afterwit

We've all had it. Someone took you by surprise and said something rude. You weren't ready. But later on, as you mulled over the conversation for the fiftieth time, you had *the best* comeback! In your head, you picture yourself delivering it. Oh, and it's good! *Take that*, you say. Only they can't hear you. They never will. It's too late. The moment has passed. It's called "afterwit": a good comeback; the retort one thinks of only after the end of a discussion or after leaving a social gathering.

Typically, there's no real pleasure in afterwit. It just haunts you. You beat yourself up for your late-to-the-party brilliance. *Why couldn't I have thought of that in the moment? Why do I always get tongue-tied at the least opportune times?*

But what if you used afterwit to intentionally improve your forewit? Forewit is the opposite: timely knowledge; precaution; foresight. You can create your own personal rules about how to respond to specific types of behavior. For example, Yvette has a strong personal boundary about respect. She will not engage in disrespectful conversation. She communicated to the person that she could resume the conversation when she calmed down. Most people who are used to controlling others through anger and belittling are not used to being shut down. That is not the response they want. It defuses their power. Rather than allowing others to push your buttons, deactivate the buttons that create automatic, counterproductive reactions.

There is a big difference between a reaction and a response. A reaction is immediate. It is a knee-jerk behavior. It is predictable. It typically reflects back what has been thrown at you. It is a mirror—complementarity at work. A response is thoughtful. It gathers information, looks at the various dynamics in a situation, and considers the situation from the point of view of others who are involved. A response thinks ahead. If I respond in this way, how will that impact the future? How will it impact my goals and objectives? Is it purposeful? Will it matter a month from now or a year from now?

If you are to speak differently, your words and tone cannot be a reaction. They must be a response. Sometimes your decision will be to remain quiet for the time being. Other times, you will say something that is completely unexpected because you have taken the time to be intentional. Some situations you inevitably face are worthy of your forewit—a decision you make in advance about how you will respond if and when the situation arises.

Besides situations such as yelling or disrespect, you may be asked questions that put you on the spot and which you may typically answer begrudgingly and inauthentically. Perhaps you have a tendency to react a particular way to a nosy question that is routinely asked in social situations (for example: "When are you going to have children?" "Do you have any job openings for my son [daughter/niece/cousin]?") Each time you are asked, you bumble your answer in some way. What if, instead, you think back to the last time that happened and use afterwit to formulate a response that you can use the next time?

What situations or questions that are likely to recur have left you tongue-tied?

Looking back with the lens of afterwit, how would you like to have responded?

How would you like to respond in similar situations in the future?

One caveat here. *Non-complementary behavior is not a solution for long-term abuse.* If you are in an abusive relationship, a situation in which you are dealing with repeated dysfunctional behavior, seek help. Non-complementary behavior is meant to break a pattern, not to form a new pattern in which you are repeatedly attacked with verbal or other assaults and respond repeatedly with kindness without mutual resolution of the problem. A non-complementary response is a tool for unique, isolated conversations—not a setup for codependent behavior.

If you are to speak differently, your words and tone cannot be a reaction. They must be a response.

Be Willing to Be Different

Yvette Cook, who dealt so effectively with the bully client who brought account executives to tears with her rants, exemplifies the sort of success this book is about. And her unique ability to communicate authentically with both power and warmth is unusually great. I have coached hundreds of individuals and trained thousands. She's at the top. She is one of the coaches I seek out when I need help communicating in a difficult scenario. So I want to share a little more of her story here to illustrate a few more insights.

I first met Yvette in my mid-twenties while running a public relations firm. She hired my business to help with a huge expo and entertainment event. When she graduated from the University of Denver in the 1980s, Yvette took a job as an assistant credit manager for department store Marshall Field's in Dallas, making $12,500 a year. "I had no car note and no credit card debt, but I was barely making it," she says. "A friend and I decided to go to grad school together, and we started a little ad agency." She returned to Denver and they ran the business while going to school. While helping clients, she met someone from a television station, and a comment he made stuck with her.

"He commented that salespeople in television made a lot of money," she remembers. She thought about it and realized she'd been selling since high school, so why not? She'd done retail and door-to-door sales. She'd even worked as a fur coat model in college. "Working in the credit department, on the sales floor, as a model. To me, it was all sales. As long as you believe in a product, you can sell it." While she knew she eventually wanted to do something in the nonprofit service arena, she began in sales because she wanted a solid financial footing for her life. That foresight turned out to be a lifesaver for her and her family. After getting married at 25 and giving birth to three children within just a few years, she found her personal life unraveling. By her early thirties, she was a divorced single mom.

"To be honest, my professional growth came from being a single mom needing to support three children," she said. "I knew it was going to be a challenge to progress in my career as a single parent. I also knew I was in an industry that would allow me to provide them things like a private education and college. When I started out in sales, that was why."

She began at a small radio station following graduate school, hoping to make a quick transition to television. She did. Three months later, she landed exactly where she had aimed, as an account executive with one of the most successful network affiliates in the country. She soon got her first promotion. Then another. "Then I hit the glass ceiling," she recalls. "It was frustrating. Up until that point, I didn't really think there were barriers. My parents had taught me and my brother that all things were possible. It was my first dose of reality that there really are ceilings."

Finding an Internal Locus of Control

Rather than respond in a way that would burn bridges, she decided to respond with a powerful question for herself and the mentors and friends outside of the station whom she trusted. "My reaction was, 'Okay, how do I work around this?'"

This response is noteworthy. She flipped the typical script—complaining and accepting the status quo—and asked a question that empowered her to turn a problem into an opportunity. It is something that successful women do consistently—focus on what they can control rather than stewing over what they can't. You'll hear it in the language they use when faced with challenges. Those who struggle to succeed will use language to complain about the situation, attempt to manipulate decision makers, or generally focus on the problem. They say things such as:

- This is a really big problem. Most people don't clear this hurdle, so I probably just need to learn to live with it.
- If no one else has overcome it, I don't know why I should think I will.
- The world is unfair. My life is unfair.
- Why can't I ever get ahead?

Successful women talk about it like this:

- I've got a problem. How do I work around it?
- Whom do I know who could help me?
- How have successful people I look up to worked around this problem?
- I will not allow what I can't control to control me.
- I will make the most of what I can control, even if that means making a big, scary change.

Locus is Latin for "location," so the idea of a locus of control is about where and what you think impacts the events of your life. People with an external locus of control blame and praise external factors for what occurs in their lives. People with an internal locus of control tend to believe that their actions largely determine the events of their life. This means that when a challenge appears, they not only see what they could have done differently that would have led to a different outcome, but they also consider what they can do now to push through the challenge.

A woman of faith can struggle with this concept if she is not balanced in her perspective. For example, if you believe God controls every aspect of what happens in your life and that it doesn't really matter what you do because things are just going to happen the way God intended, then you have an external locus of control that absolves you of any responsibility for the outcomes in your life. If this describes you, make it your goal to notice what God has put within your control to overcome your challenges. You have gifts, resources, connections. Don't waste those blessings. Use them.

Yvette did just that. "A friend who knew what I was dealing with called me about a job with Gannett," a major media company that was looking to promote women at the time. "I went into their station management fast-track program," she explained. "My children and I moved to North Carolina, and I became a general sales manager." Soon after, she was promoted to vice president.

"I wasn't trying to be promoted to VP. I came to work every day and gave it my all and tried to do my best for the organization. I think the opportunity came as a result."

She made a shift toward her original goal of nonprofit service in 1999 when she went to a public broadcasting station as vice president of development, eventually landing at United Way in 2009 as senior vice president of marketing in Atlanta. Just one year later, she was recruited to become chief executive officer at her current organization. Her advice to women, in particular, reiterates the importance of flipping the script by not following the script so many women—and men, for that matter—follow:

- If you have a difficult conversation coming up, plan it out. The first thing you should do is put yourself in the shoes of the other people involved. See it from their side and then plan your words. What might they be feeling? What is it that they want?

- Have compassion in difficult conversations. "Speak with kindness and compassion. And always end a difficult conversation with some type of solution."

- The worst thing you can do is avoid a conversation you know needs to happen. The longer you wait, the more stressed you will be. Conversation gives release and relief.

- Don't be as concerned about being heard as about contributing something of value to the conversation. Listen to all sides. Look for solutions that consider all sides. "I don't talk much. I try to listen. I'm formulating ideas in my mind. Once everyone has talked, I interject my thoughts, and they are solution-oriented."

- Speak to people with respect. Never bully. It is the most ineffective form of communication and management. "Good leaders are servant leaders. You will get more productivity from people by treating them with the same amount of respect you want."

- Have more conversations—and fewer emails and texts. "In the days before email, it forced you to have a stronger sense of personal communication and interaction. I don't respond via email to things that need real back-and-forth conversation."

- There is nothing better than the truth, even though sometimes it is painful. "They used to say around the office, 'If you don't want to know the truth, don't ask Yvette Cook.' But I would tell it in a way that was professionally well received. You must be sensitive that there are two sides, sometimes three. Don't tell people what they want to hear but what they need to hear." If you learn to speak truth out of compassion and love rather than hurt or anger, you will be amazed by the results that will unfold in your life—both professionally and personally.

- Pause before you speak. Complementary responses rely on your automatic reaction to things. It is a natural mirroring effect that you do almost without thinking. Practice pausing before reacting so you can respond in a non-complementary way.

- Speak kindly. Use a neutral or kind tone in difficult conversations. This will deescalate an emotional response.

- Keep your eye on your vision. It is easy to be thrown off course by the distractions caused by unexpected situations and conversations, but always keep your focus on where you are headed. Then choose words that lead you a step closer to your goal.

Your Script for Success

- Heighten your awareness of complementary behavior—the tendency to mirror what others say and do.

- When engaged in conflict, do not react in complementary ways. De-escalate the conflict with a non-complementary response.

- Remember to be compassionate in your speech, especially when the words that must be spoken will inevitably be difficult for the other person to hear.

Every Woman Should Know

- Speaking differently sometimes means doing the opposite of conventional thinking.

- Humans tend to mirror one another's movements and emotions. Be intentional about movements and emotions you want to reflect back to others.

- Compassion has the power to shift even the most difficult conversation.

Coach Yourself

- What aspect of this chapter most resonates with you? What step do you feel led to take as a result?

- In what relationship do you find yourself feeling a sense of afterwit? In the future, how could you flip the script when responding to this person?

- In what situation in your life would non-complementary behavior empower you to de-escalate emotional frustration rather than inflame it?

- Where do you need to exercise some self-compassion in your life right now? What would you say differently to yourself about that situation if you were to be self-compassionate?

Speak Differently

Do not respond predictably to dysfunctional situations. Break the pattern of mirroring negative behavior. Respond in a way that is the positive opposite of what is expected. Use compassion and wisdom as your guide.

HABIT FOUR

Build Trust Through Respect

*Why you need to change your language
if you want to find freedom.*

*I speak to everyone in the same way, whether he is
the garbage man or the president of the university.*
ALBERT EINSTEIN

Key Lessons

- Successful women show up for small opportunities as they do for big opportunities.

- Boundaries are your articulation of what's okay and what's not.

- Relationships open the door to your dreams. Do not take any connection for granted.

For three years after graduating from college, Kym Lee relentlessly pursued her vision of getting into law school at Georgetown University. She even landed a job at the law school to make the connections that might better her chances of getting in. But when she got there, she realized she had pursued the wrong dream.

"I remember sitting in a lecture with *Vogue* magazine hidden between the pages of one of my textbooks," she told me. In her first year, she couldn't ignore the truth. Her passion wasn't law. Her passion was all things beauty and fashion. But how do you step away from an opportunity you worked so hard for and for so long? One that offers prestige and promise? In the case of Kym Lee, you give it all up to start over. The same determination and relationship building that got her

91

into Georgetown Law could be used to begin a brand-new career from scratch. It was a bold decision. But over the last two decades as a celebrity makeup artist, she has "painted" the faces of some of the biggest names in the film, music, political, and sports world.

After abandoning law school to pursue her passion, Kym started working at the MAC (Make-up Art Cosmetics) counter. There, she was intentional about making connections that might open a door.

"Six months later, I was invited to do makeup for a music video by someone who came to the makeup counter at MAC. They asked the manager for whoever was available in the next two weeks. The manager said, 'Okay, Kym is available.' The producer was from BET [Black Entertainment Television]."

The producer liked her work and mentioned her to a family friend of his, Derrick Rutledge. "I knew who Derrick was, but I did not understand the magnitude of what he was doing at BET. I ended up being Derrick's assistant at *Teen Summit*," which was a popular show on the network. Over time, while working on just about every in-house produced show at the network and all of the network's award shows, she met hundreds of stars and the people who managed their careers.

"BET was a major milestone because when [music] artists would come, we had a reputation for having very skilled makeup artists, so they wouldn't bring their own." Even legends such as Diana Ross, Tina Turner, and Chaka Khan allowed the BET team to do their makeup, Kym explains. "Derrick set it up that way. We all painted very similarly to him," she says of Rutledge, who is now Oprah Winfrey's makeup artist. "This gave me the opportunity to build relationships."

This is critical. It can be easy to overlook what successful women do differently. It can be easy to say, "Well, she was lucky. She got to work with the best." But the real question is, *How did she come to work with the best?* No one handed her an opportunity on a silver platter. She started from scratch with no contacts. Many people go to work at the makeup counter with dreams of painting the faces on actors in major motion pictures. Very few end up actually doing it.

What I see in Kym is someone who asks, "Where can I put myself so that I can meet the people who might be able to crack a door open for me to get to my goal?" When she didn't get into Georgetown Law after graduating with honors from Bowie State University, she asked that question. And ended up landing a job at the law library. It was while there that she finally got a yes from the law school. When a random stranger asked for a makeup artist for a music video, Kym was eager to take the opportunity—and it opened the door to serve under one of the most talented makeup artists anywhere, painting the faces of some of the biggest musical entertainers in the country.

For ten years, she worked diligently at BET before expanding her opportunities to include the sports and film industries. She did so by building trust with each person she met. How? First, she developed her talent and became great at her craft. They loved the results. It's easy to recommend someone who gets results you love. Remember at the beginning of this book, I pointed out that talent and effort are important, but your voice is the missing piece? Kym's talent and effort were flawless. But it is her voice—her ability to connect and build trust through respect for her work—that catapulted her to the next level.

"My turning point was working with Venus and Serena Williams," she recalls of the magnificent tennis duo. "It was the first time I had done an athlete of their caliber and not a music artist." The opportunity came along when her name was passed along to the Williams sisters' rep, she explains. A major national magazine cover soon followed, and more and more people took notice of her artistry.

It can be easy to say, "Well, she was lucky. She got to work with the best." But the real question is, How did she come to work with the best?

"There is a calmness and a competence you have to have when you are working with people who are high impact," she says. "Confidence comes with studying your craft and knowing what you're doing. Good preparation is always going to cause folks to know they should use you. Even when I wasn't confident, I appeared confident. People trust you when you are confident. That is something I mastered in my career. I want them to know they can depend on me and that whatever I put on them is going to look great. It isn't conceit. It's confidence."

One of Kym's biggest opportunities came by accident and turned into something much bigger. Oscar-nominated actress Angela Bassett hired Kym while in DC for a conference. "When I showed up, I actually wasn't the person she thought I was," Kym remembers. She had used another artist named Kim during another trip to DC. When Kym showed up, she recalls the actress saying, "You're not Kim." Kym said, "Yes, I am." "Well, you're not the right Kim! But you're here now, so come on."

"I had studied her face before I showed up," she says of her research of pictures and magazine spreads of the actress. It was raining and dark that day, and the room didn't have as much light as Kym would have liked. "I was like, *I hope I am doing this right*. I was fumbling," Kym says. But her work was fabulous. Two weeks later, she got a call.

"Hi, Kym, this is Angela."

"I was like, Angela who? I mean, you don't expect Angela Bassett to just call you up," Kym jokes. But it was. She called to invite Kym to be her personal makeup artist in Nova Scotia for the shooting of the hit movie *Jumping the Broom*. The experience opened the door for Kym to join the union, which opened more doors in film.

Kym landed more film work, including the movie *Sparkle*, where she was the last makeup artist to work with the late Whitney Houston. In recent years, Kym's work could be seen at the Academy Awards, the Grammys, and in film and sports and music. She launched her own makeup line, Wink & Pout. And on a personal level, she finished a master's degree in divinity and is engaged to be married.

I asked Kym for her advice about communication:

- Stay in touch. Talk to clients and those who can help you. Email them, text them, even if they aren't using your services. Keep the door open. "I don't let it close."

- Kym sees her makeup chair as a ministry to listen and encourage. "I always pray before I touch someone. I am very sensitive to the Spirit. I ask for discernment and wisdom every day." Sometimes there is no time to talk. Sometimes you need to just listen.

- Your appearance is very important. If a person's first impression is that you aren't polished, you will have to overcompensate in other areas. You're good. You're talented. Why do that to yourself?

- On appearance, she suggests: "Get your brows done. Do your nails. Put on lipstick. That goes a long way. It shows that you care."

- Remember in your personal relationship with your spouse or significant other, you may have to learn to communicate differently than in the business world. Be sensitive to that.

All along the way, relationships have connected Kym to opportunity. At each step, she could have ruined an opportunity by not showing up fully for a seemingly small opportunity, or not being consistent, or treating people who didn't appear to be in charge differently than those who were obvious decision makers. But Kym stayed focused on her goal and recognized that only through strong relationships built on trust for her work and mutual respect for her clients could she achieve the vision.

Build Trust and Respect

Kym Lee's story may seem at first to be about making connections that lead to opportunities. However, dig a little deeper and you'll notice her journey is really about building trust— trust that she can be relied on to get consistent results, show up fully every time, and show real care and concern for her clients. When you speak through your actions—preparation, consistency, and conscientiousness—you build trust with people. Trust leads to greater influence and opportunities. Ask yourself, *How am I doing at building trust? Do my actions and talent cause people to trust me more—or less?*

Ultimately, trust leads to respect. And respect opens doors of opportunity. It draws others closer to you. It multiplies connections and relationships. Respect is derived from a shared understanding and honor between two people for what's acceptable and what isn't. It is about establishing the boundaries and expectations that empower a relationship to thrive and grow. When expectations aren't met and boundaries are crossed, trust is diminished. When trust is diminished, the relationship is weakened. When the relationship is weakened, success is less likely. Why? Because your success is dependent not just upon your talent and effort, but upon the people who help you, open doors for you, and want to be a part of what you are doing.

The whole point of speaking differently is to connect with people in ways that empower you to positively impact others with your purpose, be resilient, and have joy along your journey. Speaking differently builds those relationships.

Respect opens doors of opportunity.

Setting Boundaries

If respect is derived from a shared understanding and honor between two people for what's acceptable and what isn't, then at its core, respect is about setting strong, good boundaries. That means first being clear about what's okay and what isn't. Then it means communicating those boundaries clearly.

When someone crosses your boundaries, the normal reaction is anger and resentment. Oftentimes, we find ourselves resentful because we haven't verbalized those boundaries to the other person. Whether you are afraid to speak up or you simply were not clear about expectations, when you haven't communicated the boundary to the other person, it is a problem you can fix. It will take courage if you don't like speaking up, but it is necessary. While it certainly does not apply to all women, many women struggle with setting boundaries because it makes them uncomfortable, it doesn't feel "nice," or they are afraid of what others will think. But boundaries actually empower you to have strong relationships. Boundaries set expectations and an agreement about what is okay in the relationship—and what is not. It is healthy. And for any successful relationship, personal or professional, it is necessary.

When Boundaries Are Tested

"My boss throws too much on my plate, and there is absolutely no way for me to do all of it. I want to speak up, but I don't know what to say," Marci lamented. Such a scenario has come up many times during coaching sessions with clients. When the demand is impossible to achieve given the time constraints, I typically ask clients such as Marci questions that will help them put the ball back in their boss's court.

"What would happen in your meeting tomorrow morning if you said this?" I asked, and then gave her a script: "I know you want me to finish project A and project B by Wednesday. Project A is going to require at least 12 hours to complete, including calls with the client and feedback. Project B will take about 10 hours. Which one is the bigger priority?"

For most clients, this type of script works well. Rather than decide which project to prioritize and risk getting it wrong, they ask the question. They have made it clear how much time is required, thereby illustrating with clarity that there really is a dilemma and both projects cannot be accomplished within the time frame—at least not with the resources assigned to them. Clients usually come back to the next session saying the boss chose one project over the other and adjusted the timeline for the second project, or delegated some elements of the projects to other team members in order to keep things on schedule.

In Marci's case, her hard-driving boss told her she'd need to figure out how to do both, and there would be no adjustment to the timeline. "I guess you'll need to pull a couple of all-nighters," he said casually while continuing to type on his computer. He seemed to thrive on making employees anxious, exerting his authority with unrealistic deadlines. Since the pay was above average, most employees swallowed their pride and put up with it. But on this particular day, as Marci described her dilemma, she seemed to be questioning her choices.

"I'm curious, Marci," I said. "In the moment when he barely bothered to look up from his computer while you desperately sought some relief to the stress caused by such a ridiculous deadline, how did you feel?" A string of rather depressing feelings spilled forth as Marci sighed deeply in response.

"I felt unimportant. Inferior. Dismissed. Unworthy of any sort of empathy," she rattled off. "It was as though I have no value other than to get work done. So, first of all, it felt like my stress level doesn't matter. If I keel over at my desk, oh well. Then, it felt like my life belongs to the company even outside working hours. Basically, to have this job means to give up my right to control my personal time."

"That is an eye-opening observation," I said. "So what did you say in response?"

"I didn't say anything," she said in a whisper of embarrassment and frustration. "I felt stunned, and I felt too vulnerable to say what I would like to have said, you know, something bold and strong, something to stand up for myself."

"And why is that?" I asked curiously. Even though I was pretty sure I knew the answer, as a coach I have learned to never make the assumption. Oftentimes my assumption is not accurate. Unfortunately, in this instance, though, it was.

"I don't want to lose my job," she said. "So I guess I'll just have to find a way to make it not feel so stressful. Maybe I need to adjust my expectations."

"So I just want to reflect back to you what you are saying, okay?" I asked.

"Okay."

"You are in a position where you do not feel free to speak up. You must silence your own voice and accept being treated as unimportant, inferior, dismissed, and devalued. Your plan of action to deal with this is to find a way to stop being stressed about feeling unimportant, inferior, dismissed, and devalued. Is that what you just said?" I said in a completely neutral tone.

She paused for at least 15 seconds. I heard a deep breath, followed by a sigh. Then some mumbling about having hired a coach who tells her the truth. Then an ironic chuckle. "Yeah, that *is* what I just said," she admitted, almost as though she was still processing the statement.

"Is that what you really want?"

"No. It isn't. But I don't know how to change it."

Have you ever found yourself in that predicament? Stuck in a situation, knowing nothing you can say will change the position of the person with the most power in the situation? I've been there. I felt weak and overpowered. Just like Marci. That is, until it finally dawned on me that in situations such as these, a person can only have as much power over you as you give them.

When you find yourself in a situation in which your voice is silent, your needs don't matter much, and nothing you can say will change matters, then it's time to ask yourself, "Do I need to shift the balance of power in this situation?"

Here's what I mean. As long as Marci commits to her job no matter what, just because it pays more than other jobs at her level, then she must submit herself to an authority that not only controls her work hours but infringes on her personal time again and again. If she broadens her perspective about her options, she can begin to see that this job may not be worth the things she must give up—joy, self-respect, peace—in order to keep it. Once her goal becomes about having the freedom to speak up, the freedom to choose her schedule, and the freedom of financial security, her focus will change from "keeping her job" to broadening her options.

This doesn't happen overnight, but with a clear vision it can happen. And that begins with understanding your values.

A successful woman intentionally creates a set of circumstances that gives her the freedom to speak openly about her values, needs, and beliefs. An average or unsuccessful woman instead accepts circumstances that sacrifice her values, needs, and beliefs in exchange for what feels like security—whether a job, money, or a relationship.

When you find yourself in a situation in which your voice is silent, your needs don't matter much, and nothing you can say will change matters, then it's time to ask yourself, "Do I need to shift the balance of power in this situation?"

The Real Source of Freedom

The concept of creating professional and financial freedom takes a shift in mindset, whether being an in-demand free agent who never has to hunt for a job, working for yourself on your own terms, or not working at all. The first shift is to realize that a job or a person is not your source of opportunity. It is so much bigger than a person. God Himself creates opportunities, and He can create ones you never even imagined. But that usually doesn't happen until you begin to think differently about what your life, schedule, bank account, and relationships can look like. In Matthew 19:26, Jesus reminds us, "With God all things are possible."

Even for the most faith-filled woman, it is not unusual to sometimes lose sight of this truth. When life is filled with uncertainty and you've been stuck in the same spot for years, you can begin to believe that this is just the way it will be. That the best you can hope for is to make it through, pay the bills, hang on to that relationship, and be glad you have a job. But I believe you are reading these words because you are not average. There is something more and better for you. And having the freedom to make choices that reflect your faith and your potential is part of that something better.

So maybe it is time to begin imagining what might need to shift, what new choices will lay the groundwork to build a life in which you have more say about how you spend your time and who you spend it with. It may not happen overnight, but the possibility begins to unfold the day you decide that living like everyone else doesn't work for you anymore—and that maybe, just maybe, God has something better in store.

The first shift is to realize that a job or a person
is not your source of opportunity.

When I think back to the vision I first had at 20 years old—having a career as an author and being happily married with children—I realize that the life I now live began with my thoughts. By 22, I began speaking that life into existence and actively working toward it.

I attempted to write my first book at that age. I say attempted because I literally wrote all the wisdom I had and after about 10,000 words, I had absolutely nothing left to say. I hadn't gotten my purpose yet. I wasn't ready. But I was willing. Two more attempts and four years would pass before I succeeded at publishing my first book. Yes, I read the statistics that 95 percent of agents turn down aspiring authors for representation. And I knew the stats that 97 percent of manuscripts sent to publishers land in the trash bin. My curiosity was about the other 3 percent. If I could figure out what they did differently than the 97 percent, I could get published too. And if I could get published, maybe I could have a career as an author—one that would allow me the freedom to work when I wanted and not when I was told. Freedom is a core value for me, so it was my dream.

In that coaching session with Marci that day, the idea that her life could begin to look different became her dream. She got curious about what it would take to have the freedom to speak up rather than shut up when she was treated unprofessionally and unfairly on the job. Rather than focusing on the fear of losing her job and income, she began focusing on a vision of working for joy rather than money. "Passion sounds nice, but it doesn't pay the bills" was something her single mom used to say when reminiscing about how she'd once wanted to start an interior design business. Marci grew up hearing messages over and over about "getting a good job" and "being realistic." These weren't just long-held beliefs. They were words she'd repeated herself. To find freedom, she'd need to change her language.

Since you are reading this book, I'm trusting that you are open to seeing your choices in a different light too. Sometimes having the confidence and boldness to speak your truth requires you to situate yourself in an environment that is supportive of your authentic self. Otherwise, you find yourself dealing with consequences that you are not prepared to absorb.

To find freedom, she'd need to change her language.

Your turn. Identify the situation(s) in which you feel bound to stay silent, go along with an untruth, or pretend all is well when it is not.

Now, identify the most troublesome consequence of speaking up. What are you afraid will happen? If that happens, what will be the domino effect?

Sit in a quiet, peaceful spot alone. Breathe in and imagine that the air is faith and divine wisdom. Invite the Holy Spirit to reveal to you the shift that needs to occur in your life. Picture yourself free to speak the truth without the consequences having the power to frighten or devastate you. What is present in this vision that frees you to speak up?

Whatever is present in this vision that doesn't exist in your current reality is what I invite you to imagine for your life. Think boldly. Give yourself permission to dream it. Set an intention to begin taking steps toward it. Decide that the way things look today is not an indicator of the way they will look tomorrow.

Say What You Mean. Mean What You Say

What is it exactly that causes us to be anything other than authentic when we're talking to other people? I mean, when you want to express your truth, when you have something to say but you hold back, what is it that's really going on? When you meet someone new but feel you have to impress them rather than just be you and allow the opportunity to unfold organically, what is that all about? I'd like to suggest to you that oftentimes it is this: the crave for praise. That craving to be liked, to be approved of, is also known as fear of rejection, fear of disapproval, and people pleasing. If you are like many other women, this may be one of your core fears. And it can show up without your really noticing that it is driving your communication with people, or lack thereof.

We can spend so much time wanting people to like us, wanting to be accepted, wanting approval, or wanting the enviable job/spouse/whatever that it changes how we interact with people. Rather than being ourselves, we are tempted to be who we believe we must be in order to be accepted. Sometimes that means being quiet. At other times, that means maintaining the status quo and saying what people want to hear. As a result, they really can't see us—the real us. They can see only our insecurity. And when that happens, it is not pretty. When our insecurities speak, we say things we don't really mean—things we believe will win us approval and love.

What You Say	What You're Thinking
Sure, I'd love to work on that project!	I hate working on these assignments because the whole team is negative. I wish I could get reassigned to a different department so I could work with more positive people.
I'm not upset.	I am so upset right now!
Oh, no. You didn't offend me at all.	I absolutely, positively cannot believe you said that. It was insensitive and selfish and careless.
Of course you're welcome to stay! I always love having you.	I'm exhausted. I need some rest. I can't believe you can't see that.

Clear speakers are strong leaders. You'll keep yourself out of a lot of trouble and avoid misunderstandings if you boldly, but kindly, tell the truth. Say what you mean. Mean what you say. If you feel uncomfortable, you can even say so: "This is awkward to say, but…" "I've given this a lot of thought..." "What I am trying to say is..." Prefacing particularly difficult statements with an acknowledgment that you know what you are saying might be difficult to receive is a way of letting air out of a tense conversational balloon. It can ease tension for you and for the person to whom you are speaking.

Clear speakers are strong leaders.

What to Say When You're Afraid to Say No

Do you ever struggle with saying no? If you get so anxious about declining a request that you end up going against your better judgment and saying yes or avoiding the conversation altogether, here are a few ways to authentically voice exactly what you need to say.

1. **"Let me think about that."**

   Sometimes, you're just not sure you want to say yes. If it just doesn't feel right or it is a request that deserves more than a knee-jerk reaction, say, "Let me think about that and get back to you." Especially if you are someone who says yes much too quickly and ends up regretting it, this statement should become a habit. It gives you the breathing space to process the request and build the courage to be honest in your response. Then, if the answer is no, one of the next three statements can be your follow-up.

2. **"That's not going to work for me."**

   Whether it is a conflict in your schedule or a conflict in values, "That's not going to work for me" is a boundary-setting statement. It indicates that your decision is about your needs and/or boundaries. If there is a negotiation to be had about the request, it communicates that the only way to get to a yes is for the person making the request to adjust the request so that your needs are met.

3. "I wish I could say yes."

Especially when you feel badly about saying no, expressing that you wish you could say yes is a way to acknowledge this is not something you take lightly. You want to be able to help, but you simply cannot.

4. "No."

Not every no requires an explanation. Sometimes a simple "Thanks, but no thanks" is really all you need. Especially if you have a habit of saying no tacked on to a long explanation that eventually turns into a yes, try saying no and then stop yourself from saying *anything else*. "No" is a complete sentence.

    When there is a situation where you need to say no, tell the truth and just say it. When you feel afraid, remember that all you need to do—*literally*—is open your mouth and let the words come out. Trust that things will unfold as they should.

When your insecurity speaks, it doesn't always result in your "going along to get along," being agreeable by saying what you believe must be said in order to maintain the relationship, the job, or the status. Sometimes you say nothing when you really want to speak up. You've been sitting in a meeting with an idea you want to share, but rather than speak up, you shut down. Fearing rejection, you avoid disapproval by never speaking in the first place. You're so concerned about what people might think if you don't say exactly the right thing, you silence yourself.

Have you ever experienced a situation like this? Describe it below. Why did you choose not to speak? What do you wish you would have said in those circumstances?

Some of this is cultural. Historically, women were able to gain praise by being quiet, by going along. You may have been told that being meek and gentle means keeping your thoughts to yourself.

Depending on your religious upbringing, this idea may be so ingrained that you aren't always aware of how such a misinterpreted belief has affected your communication style. Perhaps the women you saw praised in your upbringing were the ones who said very little, who fit into a box of perfection in which they followed every legalistic rule that was thrust upon them. The result is often a life that looks neat and tidy from the outside, but inside there's a woman who is silently hemorrhaging from the pain of living a life that meets everyone's expectations but her own.

Begin thinking and speaking differently about yourself, and you will give life to healthy relationships and death to dysfunctional ones.

Own Your Story

Connecting with other people and building trust often begins with finding common ground. When we speak to others and when we listen to others, we are wired to find commonalities that feel familiar. Whether it is a shared experience or just a shared reaction to an experience, telling stories is a powerful way to connect. In romantic relationships, storytelling is a way that couples bond early in a relationship. Psychologists explain it is important to keep telling stories throughout the relationship as a way to strengthen the connection. Stories are intimate and so, when you are able to share your story, there is a certain vulnerability that builds just a little bit more connection. It allows the person listening to your story to understand you better.

Just as importantly, though, research shows that the way you construct your story can impact your happiness and life satisfaction.[1] Remember that success is a harmony of purpose, resilience, and joy. Storytelling, when you construct experiences of the past in a way that is positive and empowering, can have a positive impact on both your mental and physical health.

Consider the way Kym told her story of leaving law school to start over from the bottom, pursuing a career where she had to completely make her own way. She could have told the story from a more pessimistic viewpoint, beating herself up for spending three years pursuing a goal that turned out not to be her passion. I have known Kym for more than 12 years, and I have never heard her speak of her experience negatively. She frames it in terms of discovering her passion. She thought she wanted law, but she was miserable. She mustered the courage to let that inauthentic dream go. We all have challenges, failures, and false starts. The question is, How can you tell the story of your life in a way that honors how your journey has made you wiser or better?

You can't be powerful and play the victim simultaneously. Own your story. Tell it powerfully and truthfully. Think of your life as a novel. The stories you tell make up the chapters, and the new chapters are unfolding as we speak. If not for some of the bad chapters, you would not have made it to the good chapters. Novels are boring when there is no plot twist, no challenge, no moral of any sort. Being intentional about how you tell your story means looking at your life through the lens of an observer who is rooting for you to win, empathetic when you fall, and can laugh at moments of utter ridiculousness.

Let's stop here for a moment so you can consider your story. Or rather, identify a vivid, specific moment in your life that stands out for some reason—whether it was a proud moment or a funny one, a difficult moment or an epiphany. Bullet point here the beginning, middle, and end of the story. What led to it? What happened? How did you respond? What were the consequences or lessons learned?

If you want to go deeper with your story, journal about it exactly as you want to tell it in future conversations, using the bullet points above as your guide.

You can't be powerful and play the victim simultaneously.

Authenticity

Deep down, we all want to belong. It is a longing for love, a basic human need. And when we don't experience love in healthy ways, we seek counterfeit versions of it. As you deepen your understanding that you are embraced and accepted exactly as you are by the One who created you, your need to hide who you are and fear disapproval begins to melt. Receiving the truth of your own divinely ordained worth and value gives you courage to be yourself.

Do you accept you? It isn't just the rejection by other people that influences what we say and how we say it. It is also our rejection of ourselves. When you don't see yourself as acceptable, as worthy of being heard, you sabotage your own ability to speak truthfully and boldly in your relationships and work. The truth is, the pain of rejection can cause us to begin seeing ourselves through other people's lenses rather than God's lens. You can jump on board with their assessments and open up a cycle of self-loathing that shapes how you communicate.

In this cycle, you can choose relationships that reaffirm the viewpoint that you are not acceptable or worthy of good opportunities. Your communication style will broadcast your insecurities and attract people who thrive on those insecurities. So you'll wonder why you seem to end up with friends who don't support you or aren't happy for your success. You'll be frustrated by romantic relationships with men who seem to take for granted your kindness, generosity, and other beautiful qualities. But step back and look at the situation from a different perspective, and you'll see that the relationships you allow into your life simply reflect what you are willing to put up with based on what you believe you deserve. Change your beliefs about yourself, and you'll transform your interactions with people.

Life and death, literally, are in the power of the tongue. Begin thinking and speaking differently about yourself, and you will give life to healthy relationships and death to dysfunctional ones.

Truly love yourself—and embrace God's love toward you—and your need for authenticity grows even stronger. Opportunities you once craved because of the praise that accompanied them will cease to matter so much to you. "Perfect love casts out fear," 1 John 4:18 (NKJV) states. The love of God and your love for yourself will literally cast out your fear of rejection and your addiction to approval and validation.

Authenticity can also change your perception of a "big" opportunity. I saw this happen in my own life a few years ago.

I'd just left the office for the day. I sat down in the driver's seat, buckled my seatbelt, and pulled out my phone. I wanted one last check of my email before pulling out of the parking lot. Three messages had appeared since I'd last checked, and one of them was an unfamiliar name with an intriguing subject line. It suggested that whoever the person was, she was seeking a life coach for a new show on one of the major networks.

Now, to put this into context, I have received quite a few inquiries over the years from production companies pitching new shows to networks and looking for a host with a background in life coaching or psychology. I've shot pilots. I've flown to Los Angeles for meetings. I've been the chosen host. I've even hosted two television shows on cable networks. But this was different. It was an executive from a major network contacting me about a show that was already greenlighted.

Before I knew it I was flying to New York for an interview and screen test. It went very well. So well that it was down to just me and one other candidate. As my attorney and manager negotiated with network executives on my behalf, I imagined how my life was going to change. This was just the kind of opportunity I had dreamed of, and it was on the verge of coming to life...if I could just make it one more step.

Have you ever been close to victory, yet it wasn't quite yours yet? You can't stop daydreaming. On many occasions during this period, I closed my eyes and imagined my plans unfolding. I would get an apartment in New York and keep my place in Atlanta. I was single at the time so there were no family commitments. I thought of my New York friends I'd spend more time with. I imagined how this would expose my books to so many more people. And I was in awe of God—look at what He was doing! You want to have faith to believe while not becoming so overwhelmed by the possibility that it would devastate you if it fell through. That's where I was. One step away from my television dream. One step away from a daily daytime series where I could contribute to helping women transform their lives. This was the opportunity that would catapult me to the next level. This might just be divine destiny.

The energy was intense. The network had a specific image in mind of who they wanted for this particular cohost slot. And I wanted to be the person they were looking for.

The moment of truth came the day I sat in front of a group of network and production company executives. I didn't pick up on the series of questions they asked at first, but looking back, I realized they were trying to figure out if I have the stereotypical background they expected from someone who looks like me.

I began to pick up on it through some of the feedback I received throughout the process. Apparently, they weren't just looking for a life coach. They were looking for a woman of color. But they wanted a woman of color that fit their image of what a woman of color is supposed to act like on television. So while they wanted professional credentials and a certain educational background, they also wanted a stereotype…and I didn't fit their stereotype.

After another interview and screen test I had the opportunity to try to force my dream to come true. I could have chosen the inauthentic path—fitting into the box that was prepared for the person who would ultimately fill the role.

I decided not to. In the end, the other candidate made the same choice. At the last hour, after countless conversations and interviews, the executives chose an entirely new candidate who had not been a part of the months-long process but fit the image of who they were looking for.

Here's what I realized. I am who I am. If I have to become some-one else in order to be successful, then it is not me who is successful. It is a poor imitation of me. And eventually, I'll get exhausted pretend-ing to be someone else just to get the attention and praise that comes with the spotlight. If such an opportunity is meant to be, surely God will open the door uniquely created for my gifts and personality. And if it is not meant to be, why would I want it other than for the acco-lades and bragging rights?

How can you tell the story of your life in a way that honors how your journey has made you wiser or better?

Remember this: *Success is a harmony of purpose, resilience, and joy.* If an opportunity requires you to communicate an image of who you are that is not in line with your purpose, does not empower your resil-ience, or does not tap into joy, it is not the right opportunity for you.

When I got the news from the network, I should have been dev-astated. The excitement of an opportunity with a major network had been a whirlwind. But I was caught off guard by a feeling of relief. Being sized up and evaluated and coached to fit into a box is awful. You know what it conjures up for me—and perhaps for you too? It conjures up feelings of not being good enough, of always needing to do some-thing more to be acceptable. And in that place, we cannot live in the fullness of who God created us to be.

I thought I wanted that job, but my soul didn't want that job. My soul knew I'd have to work too hard to be someone else. And once you sign up for that, when does it end? You become more and more in demand for being a fraud. You have to keep it up. Eventually, you lose yourself. Stay true to who you are, and I believe the right opportuni-ties—the ones you can live at peace with—will unfold.

Your Script for Success

- The next time you have a seemingly small opportunity, show up as though it's the opportunity you've been waiting for. It just might be.

- Set high standards for yourself, your behavior, and your work. When you live up to such standards, it builds trust.

- Be willing to make a major change, if needed, in order to have relationships rooted in trust and respect.

Every Woman Should Know

- Relationships matter. Success does not happen in a vacuum.

- Boundaries empower strong relationships and set the expectations for what is acceptable and what isn't.

Coach Yourself

- In an area where you have a goal yet to be reached—whether relational, financial, professional, or otherwise—ask yourself this: What are your personal minimum expectations for your behavior? What do you want these standards to "speak" about you?

- What opportunity do you have coming up that seems small? What would it look like to show up for this opportunity in a big way?

- Boundaries are about respect. What boundary do you need to set in an area where you haven't verbally expressed your boundary?

Speak Differently

Make it your goal to connect authentically with people so you can build trust. When others trust you because of your high standards, doors of opportunity begin to unfold.

Ask Powerful Questions

*Why you should be less concerned about
finding the right answers and more concerned
about finding the right questions.*

To raise new questions, new possibilities,
to regard old problems from a new angle,
requires creative imagination.

ALBERT EINSTEIN

Key Lessons

- In school, rewards come from getting the right answers. In life, the biggest rewards come from asking the right questions.

- You don't have to feel courageous to be courageous. Open your mouth and kindly say what needs to be said.

- Listening is a key to knowing what to ask.

I sat next to him on the sofa in my bright fuchsia top with lipstick to match. I'd spent 45 minutes getting my curls to cooperate before he rang the doorbell to pick me up for a company holiday party. I felt I knew his coworkers because we chatted about them so much, but I had never met any of them. I was kind of looking forward to it but beginning to wonder what the point would be. The spark that had been there a year earlier when I'd thought, maybe, finally, maybe, this is the one—it barely flickered anymore.

The light of that spark had been extinguished for months by a force I couldn't explain. He couldn't explain it either, except to say that it felt like an internal psychological struggle. I was supportive. I listened. I encouraged. But he had pulled further and further away. And it was the same behavior he admitted he'd had in past relationships. It was becoming apparent this wasn't going to work out long term, but when I prayed about it, I got this distinct message from the Holy Spirit: Don't break up with him. Let him break it off.

It had been about three months since that message came to me, and my spirit was weary. I had a clear vision of the kind of relationship and marriage God wanted for me, and at this point, I was increasingly skeptical that it would ever evolve from this particular relationship.

So as we sat there on the sofa, discussing something problematic he'd said earlier that day, I silently prayed for the right words to speak. I looked at my watch. We'd need to leave soon. I wanted just the right question that would jolt us out of this stuck place. To be honest, I wasn't looking forward to starting over—again. I don't like dating. I had prayed one specific prayer consistently after healing from a divorce: "Lord, if the guy is not 'the one,' please don't let it last past one or two dates."

I was serious about that prayer. I would rather have been alone than dating someone indefinitely if it wasn't leading to marriage. I knew what I wanted for my life: a happy, purposeful marriage with someone I love and adore who loves and adores me and with whom I share a common vision for life and a family of our own. In my late thirties, I didn't feel I had a whole lot of time to waste dating someone for a year if it wasn't going in that direction.

I took a deep breath. The words came to me. In a tone that was kind and genuinely curious, I turned my head and looked directly into his eyes. "If you had the courage, what would you do about our relationship?"

He hesitated maybe two seconds before saying the most honest thing I had heard in months: "I would step away from the relationship and work on myself."

As soon as he said it, I physically experienced what felt like release in my spirit—almost like a rope that had been stretched to capacity finally popped right inside my chest. It was the strangest sensation—sad and happy at the same time. My emotions were hurt and upset. But my spirit was free and light. "Well, that answers it, then, doesn't it?" I said quietly. There was nothing more to discuss. We needed to move on.

I didn't break up with him. I asked a powerful question. There could be no story about how I walked away. By answering the question honestly, he had to own the ending of the relationship. I don't know why God wanted it that way, but He did.

I called one of my best friends, and she arrived in less than 15 minutes, irritated and consoling. "He could have figured this out six months ago!" she fussed. She was right. But hey, at least it wasn't six more months. That night, I cried. I prayed. I rehashed conversations and all that had transpired over the previous year until my eyelids couldn't stay open and I involuntarily drifted off to sleep.

Amazingly, when I awoke the very next morning, there was an inexplicable joy in my soul. I opened my Bible and read. I sat on my living room floor and stretched and meditated. I felt so light, I thought I might float away. It made absolutely no sense. All I can say is that I had the distinct feeling that this was the start of a new chapter in my life.

And you know what? It was. My spirit knew what I could not yet see in the natural. The vision that was planted in my heart for marriage and family was about to unfold, and the powerful question I had asked the night before was meant to clear the path for the right relationship to develop in my life. I needed a little time to recuperate, but within a few months my husband—the man I love and adore and who loves and adores me—stepped into my life.

In the grand scheme of my life, it could be easy to overlook the significance of that one moment, that one question. A part of me really didn't want to ask the question because I already knew what the answer would be. A part of me did not want to start over again, did not want to try dating again—just wanted the relationship to work already.

I didn't want to deal with the aftermath, having to muster more faith to keep believing for something that was increasingly looking like more of a fantasy than a vision. I was almost 40 and believing for marriage and family. Maybe settling for a mediocre relationship would be better than nothing at all. I mean, it would be nice to have someone to go out with, to double-date with. It wasn't like he was a bad guy; he just wasn't the guy for me.

Here's where the critical moment can pass us by. In the heat of the moment, when it would be easier to stay quiet, to pretend things are okay, and to let our fears and doubts rule what comes out of our mouths—this is where we are most likely to get tripped up. I believe it was the strength that came from praying in that moment that led me to open my mouth and ask, "If you had the courage, what would you do about our relationship?"

I could have easily been just as passive in that conversation as he had been up until the moment of truth. Then what would have happened? We would have headed to the office party, smiled and laughed like nothing was wrong, and who knows how much more time would have passed before things ended? In fact, when God's chosen man for me came along, I might have been busy wasting my time with someone else. But I wasn't. All because of the courage to ask a powerful question.

Where does this apply in your life right now? What question do you need to ask? Maybe it is in a relationship. Perhaps it is at work. Perhaps you need clarity about a financial arrangement. Or you need to have a conversation with a family member.

I was trained first as a journalist and years later as a personal coach. At the core of both is the necessity to ask powerful questions that get to the truth of a matter and move the conversation forward. At the Coaching and Positive Psychology Institute, we teach "Powerful Questioning" as a core competency for any effective personal or executive coach. I want to stop for a minute and say this: Powerful Questioning is a core competency for any successful woman. Here's why:

- Asking powerful questions eliminates confusion. It keeps you from making assumptions or jumping to incorrect conclusions, thereby saving you a lot of time, energy, and misguided relationships.

- Asking powerful questions empowers others to own their actions and keeps you from being overresponsible. You can tell others what to do or you can help them find the right answer. The answer they come to on their own is usually more powerful because they are responsible for it.

- Asking powerful questions stimulates ideas. If you feel pressure to always have all the answers and ideas, asking powerful questions is a tool you can use to invite others into the creative process rather than going it alone.

- Asking powerful questions is a way to set clear boundaries. Rather than assume others understand your boundaries, make them clear and ask if they agree to those boundaries. If they don't, that is your starting point for deeper conversation.

- Asking powerful questions empowers you to make requests of people. You can alleviate a lot of stress simply by making requests and "delegating by asking."

- Asking powerful questions is how you unearth your mission and your vision. How is someone's life better when they cross your path? That's your mission. What do you want your life to look like at a given point in the future? That's your vision. Whether you are figuring out your own vision or helping someone else uncover theirs, it begins with the questions you ask.

- Asking powerful questions can create big shifts. Most people remain stuck because they have not been challenged with the kinds of questions that will propel them to the next level. The one right question can change your life.

The Courage to Ask Powerful Questions

Really powerful questions can be scary. They can lead to answers we feel we are not ready to hear. They can be uncomfortable. They can lead to breakups. They can cause people to make major changes. But those are the pivotal moments that make the difference between success and mediocrity.

If you want success at the next level, you must be willing to ask powerful questions. And that means pushing through your fears. It means getting comfortable with being uncomfortable. It means being willing to sacrifice the status quo in favor of the truth. It means operating with courage.

So just how do you do it? Where do you find the courage and how do you strengthen it?

Pray for It

In my own experience, one of the fastest routes to courage has been prayer. Getting quiet and centered and asking for the strength and courage to pose a difficult question has always elevated me to a place of greater boldness. When asking a powerful question in your own strength leaves you feeling paralyzed to speak up, remember that there is a strength much greater than your own at work. Tap into it, and you'll be amazed at the powerful words that will come out of your mouth.

Plan for It

Many critical conversations are not spontaneous conversations. When you have a meeting, an appointment, a presentation, or a lunch date with a friend with whom you've been needing to chat, don't wing it.

What is the purpose of the conversation? What do you need to know that you currently don't know? How can you be of service to the person (or people) on the other side of the conversation? What do you need them to do or to understand? Get clarity before the conversation begins. Pinpoint problems and opportunities you want to address. Doing so will diminish your fear as you identify ahead of time the obstacles you must address.

Call Out Your Fears

One of the fastest ways to overcome fear is to acknowledge it. So often we pretend not to feel fear and to try to brush it aside, which only makes it grow as an obstacle.

Call it out. Say it out loud: "I am afraid that if I ask this question, I won't get the answer I want." "I am afraid that if I ask that question, I'll be seen as rude or pushy." "I am afraid to ask for what I want because I think I'll be rejected and feel unworthy all over again." "I'm afraid to ask the question because I don't think they want to answer it, and I don't want to make them uncomfortable."

Honestly state your fears. Then ask, "And what if that happens? What will I do then?"

Take Courage

You don't have to feel courageous to be courageous. The most successful people don't necessarily feel less fear. The difference is that they don't act on their fears.

When Should I Use Powerful Questions?

I am a natural questioner. I am curious. And I seek to know the purpose of just about everything. I don't even think about it. It is just how my brain works. I notice things and ask, "Hmm. I wonder why..."

Sometimes this can work to my detriment, as even my own mother has pointed out on multiple occasions. When I was about five years old and we lived in Florida, we took a trip to Disney World with friends and family. I loved Mickey and Minnie Mouse and all of the Disney characters, and I was beyond excited to see them in person. As the Disney characters approached while we stood on the sidelines of a parade, all of the children became excited and animated, jumping up and down yelling, "Mommy! Daddy! It's Mickey! Look, it's Miccckkkkey!"

My mom looked down to notice I was less than enthused. My arms were crossed, and I looked upset. "Val! Look! It's Mickey!" she said, trying to muster up some excitement.

I looked up at her to explain the problem since clearly she hadn't noticed. We had been duped. "That's...not...Mickey!" I explained. "Look at those legs! Those are people legs! That is not Mickey!"

Not content to take the characters at face value, I examined them carefully and decided that Mickey must be taking the day off and somebody had dressed up as Mickey to take his place. That, according to my mother, was the day she realized my questioning of things could spoil my own fun. This was the moment she knew I was too curious for my own good. All of that to say, there are times when it is possible to overdo your curiosity. When it's time to relax and enjoy a fun time, for example.

Every topic does not need to be followed by a question. Be genuine, but be cognizant of asking too many questions, especially back-to-back. Powerful questioning is not the same as powerful interrogation. If a person is left feeling accused, badgered, or violated in some way by your questions, your conversation with them will do more harm than good.

Be intentional about asking powerful questions when…

- you want to find the right solution to a problem
- you want to help someone navigate a challenge or opportunity
- you want to better understand something or someone
- you want to gain the help of other people to reach a goal
- you sense there is something more to learn

Sometimes, in the course of conversation, you just feel curious about something. It may not even seem logical. You have a hunch, a spiritual inkling about something. And if you ignore it, there's a good chance you'll regret it.

Think back to a dilemma in which you had a "feeling" something was up, but you ignored what you knew in your spirit was off and later regretted it.

At other times, you may be curious, but it isn't necessarily spiritual. You may be curious about the way a person went about a task or about why they are so passionate about their work. And by asking a few questions, you stumble upon a tidbit that unlocks the door to a whole new world. Asking powerful questions is not an excuse to be nosy but an invitation to be genuinely interested in others and genuinely confident in yourself.

You don't have to feel courageous to be courageous.

How Do You Know What to Ask?

At the end of this chapter, I am going to share a list of powerful questions for various scenarios. But before I give you a list, I'd like to encourage you to develop your ability to create powerful questions. The most powerful questions have eight traits in common.

Curious. The most powerful questions come from a place of curiosity inspired by a desire to understand or resolve an issue. Curiosity focuses on learning and solving more than being right or proving a point. As a result, when you ask a question from a place of curiosity, it is easier to create a safe space for the other person or people involved to answer.

Hone in on what is most important. There are always peripheral issues. Focus on what matters most. Otherwise, you'll find the conversation veering down paths that do not address the core issue.

Succinct. A powerful question is not a long question. It does not require three paragraphs to lead up to it. The average seventh grader ought to understand your question. Short and sweet is powerful. Here's why: When a question gets long, the people being asked have to remember the statements that preceded it. As they attempt to hold on to the lead-up to your question, they often become confused. Besides not making your questions so long they become ineffective, give the people a chance to answer the question before you jump to the next one. There's nothing like asking a follow-up question to water down the impact of asking your initial question. Be succinct.

Direct. A powerful question leaves no room for misunderstanding. It is direct. It does not tiptoe around issues. This does not mean it is rude or abrupt. It simply means your question is bathed in truth and authenticity. If your core fear is disapproval or rejection, this might be a struggle for you. You may have learned to avoid the truth if it is uncomfortable. Use this as an opportunity to practice courage. Be direct but kind.

Reveal the person to themselves. A powerful question is powerful because it uncovers information, insights, and points of discovery that were previously buried. Sometimes the thing everyone else can see, they can't see—until a powerful question opens their eyes.

Shift your perspective. Sometimes it isn't so much that the question reveals the person to themselves, but it reveals the person to *you*. Things you may not have understood suddenly become clear. You begin to know the person on a different level. Or you begin to understand the subject matter on a different level. Your perspective is shifted.

Open up the conversation rather than closing it down. Generally speaking, open-ended questions are more powerful than closed-ended questions that lead to one-word answers such as "yes," "no," or "good." The goal of a powerful question is to move the conversation forward in a meaningful way. You can do that more quickly with questions that invite a person to share their insights, feelings, and thoughts. So "What do you think might be the next best step?" is better than "So do you agree that the next best step should be 'X'?" Not only does the latter question invite a yes or no answer, but it could steer the person toward an answer they might not otherwise give. It could also keep them from sharing a brilliant idea that might be even better than the one you presented—an idea they would have shared if you had asked the open-ended question instead.

Light and neutral. This does not necessarily mean the subject matter feels light and neutral. In fact, the heavier the subject matter, the more important it is to ask the question in a light and neutral way. Notice, I didn't say make serious subject matter funny or make light of a serious matter. I said *the way in which the question is asked* is light and neutral. This takes practice. Once you are able to pull it off, you'll find that people will sometimes talk about even the most difficult of subjects with you. Why? Because when the space in which you discuss a matter is light and neutral—without judgment, without fear—it feels as if that space has the capacity to handle something heavy. The more fear that surrounds a topic, the more important it is that there is a safe space in which to discuss the topic without negative consequence. So practice your tone of voice and voice inflection for asking powerful questions. Practice speaking calmly, maintaining neutral, soft body language and a tone of voice that does not give away your opinions about the topic—all of which can influence how a person responds to your question.

In coaching, powerful questions lie at the heart of a coach's ability to serve as a catalyst to help others get unstuck, gain clarity, and create an effective plan of action. There will be times when learning how to "coach" others can greatly contribute to your own success. Coaching skills can empower you to help people move from where they are to where they want to be. So any woman who has such skills at her disposal adds value to a conversation.

But be careful. People don't always want to be coached. They aren't always looking for you to help them find an answer. And frankly, some people are not ready to change. No number of powerful questions will force someone to make changes they don't want to make.

It is not enough to speak differently by asking powerful questions. In order to ask powerful questions, you must listen actively—with your mind, body, and spirit.

Listening—Mind, Body, and Spirit

It is impossible to ask powerful questions without being a genuine listener.

Early in my coaching career, I was taught the importance of eliminating all distractions before a coaching call. So as I got ready to answer a client call, I had a mental checklist of distractions to eliminate: Shut down the computer. Check. Close the door. Check. Remove clutter from my desk. Check. Take a moment to close my eyes, breathe, pray, and quiet my mind. Check.

But as I became more effective at coaching, I noticed myself starting to slip. Thinking that I didn't need to follow the rules precisely, my checklist began to fade away. That is, until one day when I found myself in an unusual position—grasping for questions to ask a client. This had never happened to me, not since my initial training when I was nervous about finding the perfect question for every step of a coaching conversation. What had gone wrong?

Embarrassing as it is to admit, I wasn't listening well. I mean, I heard everything that client had said, but I also heard an email chime on my computer—the computer that should have been shut down. I made the mistake of glancing over at it and could see it was from someone I had been waiting to hear back from about an important transaction. I closed the computer immediately, but now I was curious about what the email said. I looked at the clock. It would be 25 minutes before I could find out. Then a text message came in on my phone. Again, my curiosity was piqued. Just a glance wouldn't hurt, right? A friend was texting a question about dinner plans.

These things happened over the course of just two minutes! And they utterly broke my concentration. For the sake of the conversation at hand, I stepped out of my office and into the backyard, where I could bask in the beauty of sunshine and listen without interruption. Suddenly, my "split curiosity" was gone. Split curiosity is when we should be curious about the situation and people in front of us, but interruptions steal that curiosity and attempt to redirect our attention elsewhere. It is a symptom of nonlistening. It is a battle inside your mind for your attention.

When most of us think of listening, the first thing we think of is hearing what someone said. But mindful listening requires hearing, processing, and curiosity about what's been said and even what's not been said. Mindful listening notices the nuances in how someone said something. Were they getting quiet? Were they talking quickly and excitedly? Were they hesitant? The answers to those questions reveal a lot of information.

Be curious about more than the words spoken. Mindful listening also notices volume and tone of voice, warmth, and credibility. In other words, to be mindful is to hear and see and feel what is said. It is to notice what wasn't said that you would have expected to be said. And to be curious about it. Whether in a negotiation or a conversation with a friend, listen mindfully.

It is impossible to ask powerful questions
without being a genuine listener.

There is a second tool to use when listening that will empower you to ask powerful questions: your body. Our mind and emotions impact our physiological state. One of the reasons we use the phrase "Go with your gut" is because you can literally feel good and bad right there in your gut. Butterflies in your stomach due to excitement and an upset stomach due to nervousness are physiological responses to information in your environment. And when you are listening to other people, your body hears what's being said and responds. Whether you feel tightness in your shoulders because a situation is causing you stress or extra energy that boosts your confidence, pay attention to how you feel physically during a conversation. Sometimes it can reveal words and situations to be curious about.

Besides listening with your mind and body, the third component of listening comes from the spirit. Those divine nudges you sense when you are quiet enough to listen are the Holy Spirit's way of communicating to you what you might not otherwise know from pure logic. Sometimes it is a confirmation. Other times it is a warning. Pay attention.

Not only is it important to listen with your spirit, but also to use prayer and meditation as a means to know what to say and when to say it. Don't lean entirely on your personal understanding of matters. Seek answers and guidance through prayer. Some of your most powerful questions will come in this way.

Powerful Questions

There are many scenarios in which asking powerful questions will make you more successful—more purposeful, resilient, and joyful. Here are some scenarios to consider—situations in which you need to use powerful questions.

When someone just wants to complain and talk about what they don't want and don't like:

I hear what it is that you don't want. Tell me, What is it that you do want?

What do you want to see happen next?

When someone is beating around the bush and you'd like them to be straight with you:

> What is it that you're *not* saying?

When you have a chance to ask anything of a mentor or someone who has "been there, done that":

> What do you wish you had known when you were at my stage that you know now?

When someone is plagued by fear and "what if" questions that are keeping you both stuck:

> What are you afraid will happen? What if that happens? How would you overcome it?

When you want to learn something interesting about a friend or family member:

> What was your proudest moment? What did you learn from that experience?

> What is your favorite travel experience so far? What made it your favorite?

When you want to help someone boost their spirit:

> What's your favorite moment so far this week?

When you want to inspire someone toward their potential:

> Looking back ten years from now, what will you wish you had done?

When in a relationship that seems stalled:

> What does your gut tell you about this relationship right now?

When someone is wasting time beating themselves up:

> If you had a friend who talked to you the way you talk to yourself, how long would you keep that friend around?

When you want to find out what you should do more of in your marriage:

> What is your favorite thing that I do for you? What makes you feel most loved?

When you considering taking on more responsibility so you can earn more money:

> What will more money give you that you don't have right now?

When starting off a team meeting at work or a family meeting at home:

> What "win" did you have since the last meeting?

When ending a team meeting at work or family meeting at home:

> What activity are you most looking forward to this week? Why?

Your Script for Success

- Be curious. Ask the question that your spirit is wondering about—the one that may not even seem relevant but somehow keeps nudging to be asked.

- When you ask a question, stop talking. Give the other person the space to answer. Truly listen to what they are saying.

- Peel back the layers of a problem by asking questions to help you better understand it. Only then can you arrive at the right solution or answer.

Every Woman Should Know

- One powerful question can change the direction of your life, your relationships, and your career.

- What makes a question "powerful" is its ability to get to

the essence of a matter and move a conversation forward in an authentic way.

- Knowing the right question to ask often comes from listening more, not speaking more.

Coach Yourself

- Consider the most pressing dilemma you face right now. What is the most powerful question you need to answer?

- Rather than trying to fix the problem in front of you right now, make a list of powerful questions that would be wise to ask about the situation.

- It takes courage to ask powerful questions. But if you are courageous, you'll move toward authentic success—that place that is your most purposeful, resilient, and joyful. To push through your fear, ask yourself, "What am I afraid will happen if I ask the question I am afraid to ask? What if the thing I am afraid of actually happened—what would I do then?" Asking "what if" is a powerful tool for recognizing that you ultimately will be able to handle it. Most of the time, our "what ifs" never happen. They are often not even rational. Answer your "what if" questions and then move forward with courage.

Speak Differently

Go into every conversation open to learning and growth. The most successful people are curious. Recognize that through powerful questions you obtain the answers that will guide you onto the right path.

Ask for What You Want

How underestimating your value
is undermining your goals.

If you don't ask, the answer is always no.
NORA ROBERTS

Key Lessons

- The infamous wage gap is partly due to women not negotiating for higher salaries.
- Asking for what you're worth only works when you accurately perceive your worth.
- Use immediate, involuntary responses to your advantage.

An old acquaintance, DeAnn, called one day for advice about how to garner more opportunities to speak to corporations. Specifically, she needed to respond to a request from a company that offered the potential for her to do a lot more work in the future, and she wanted to do everything possible to land the gig.

"I have gotten a few opportunities with big companies, but not as many as I'd like," she explained. "A couple of times, I've actually had the feeling that my fee scares them away. I wonder how much I'd need to lower it to get more work."

Intrigued at how much she must be commanding to scare off some of the Fortune 500 companies she mentioned, I decided to get personal and broach the topic by asking for specifics. "How much are you charging?" I asked.

She shared the amount with me, sounding almost apologetic. No question, the amount was more than many people will ever make in a day. But for the work she's doing, it was a starter fee. Still, she spoke about it being too much. "And that's only for an hour of work," she continued in a concerned voice. "A friend of mine in the business suggested that amount for me, and that's what I've been going with."

I paused for a moment, searching for the right words for my response. I wanted to confirm her suspicion. My inkling was this: She *was* scaring off the big companies. But not for the reason she imagined. With her experience and background—she'd done some pretty high-profile work in her career—her problem wasn't that she was charging too much. She was charging too little. And it was undermining her credibility. Companies expected someone of her caliber to charge more. And since she didn't, they questioned whether she was really as good as they thought she might be.

"You should triple your fee," I said emphatically.

Silence.

"Within a couple of years, and with the right enhancements to your presentation, you may be able to quadruple or quintuple it," I confirmed.

"What?" she asked, perplexed.

"I think your problem is that you've priced yourself too low for your experience and background. You bring a lot to the table, and you are what they are looking for. Believe me, there are plenty of people with less to offer whom they've paid more."

"Really?" she asked, sounding timid but intrigued. "But how do I say that? What if they balk?"

"They won't," I said. "If they don't have it in the budget, they'll tell you, and they'll ask if you can do it for less. If you can, then you can agree to it, but it will still be more than the original number you gave me."

Scared but brave, she responded to the potential client, asking for the highest fee she'd ever quoted. They didn't bat an eye. She was astonished.

From that point forward, she began commanding higher rates. Her income doubled within a year. A couple of years later, she said she'd had more opportunities than ever before with some of the big companies she'd dreamed about serving for years. The biggest surprise to her was that the response she'd described as "scaring companies off" didn't seem to happen anymore.

Click, Whirr

What happened to my acquaintance DeAnn is most likely a result of something Arizona State University professor Robert Cialdini, author of the classic bestseller *Influence: Science and Practice*, refers to as the *click, whirr* response. The formal name is "fixed-action patterns," and it refers to automatic reactions that occur in response to certain stimuli.

In the animal world, researchers have discovered behaviors that occur in nearly the same order and patterns every single time. From mating rituals to maternal instinct and combat behaviors, certain animals respond the same way each time a particular trigger feature appears. It is as though the patterns are recorded on a mental "tape" that replays in the animal's mind. The "click" is a situation that calls for a particular behavior, such as defending one's territory. With the click, the tape is activated, and then, "whirr," a predictable set of behaviors unfolds.

In the early twentieth century, a new field called ethology—the study of how animals behave in their natural environment—gave understanding to this phenomenon of automatic behavioral responses. One of the most famous studies became known as the "Pavlovian response."

Russian physiologist Ivan Pavlov began a set of experiments after noticing that when he was about to give a dog powdered meat, it would begin salivating *before* it actually received the food. Salivation, of course, occurs to help with digestion, so it was curious that saliva was produced even though there was no actual food to digest yet. The mere anticipation of food triggered an automatic response in the dog. As an experiment, Pavlov began ringing a bell before he gave meat to the dog. In doing so, the dog associated the sound of the bell with the beginning of a meal. After doing this a few times, he noticed that he could get the dog to salivate by ringing the bell, even if there was no food. The bell became the trigger feature.

This type of classical conditioning can be seen throughout the animal kingdom.

Scientists began to wonder if *click, whirr* responses were specific to animals or if we, as humans, have *click, whirr* responses as well. It turns out, we do. Although we don't always respond in automatic ways, in many, many situations we do. (Think you're free of such responses? Consider what you do when someone extends a hand in greeting. Or when you feel your phone vibrate in your pocket. Or when you hear a baby cry.)

I believe such was the case with my acquaintance who called up for advice about her aspirations to present at major corporations. What was the *click, whirr* response in that situation? Corporations looking to book someone of her caliber expect to pay a certain fee for her services. The fee is confirmation in their minds of the value they will receive. This is not to suggest that such confirmation will prove to be accurate. It is simply to say that there is an automatic tendency to believe that if a product or service costs more, it must be better. We've all heard the phrase "you get what you pay for." Well, if you don't have to pay much, even if the value delivered exceeds that of someone who charges even more, the perception can be, "She must not be that good. Otherwise, she'd charge more."

The person making a decision about who to bring into the company is a human being, not a corporate entity. That person's reputation is on the line. If the speaker does well, the decision maker will be the hero. "Wow! She was awesome. Where'd you find her?" will be the glowing feedback. But if the speaker isn't up to standard, the decision maker may look like she made a poor choice. And on top of the negative feedback, it will appear that she missed an obvious clue in the process. "That's all she charged? You should have known."

When DeAnn started to charge more, she influenced decision makers by the message she spoke through her higher fees. She created a *click, whirr* response.

Take the Initiative

Meg had just been offered her first job out of college. The company had a great reputation, the work sounded challenging but exciting, and the position had great opportunity for growth. This would be a great place to launch her career.

The only problem? The starting salary was lower than she'd hoped.

Meg was nervous. She knew she ought to speak up, but she didn't want to come across as ungrateful or overly aggressive—two worries that tend to be more prevalent among women than men. With knots in the pit of her stomach and a twinge of guilt in her tone, she mustered the courage to speak up when it was time to talk to Human Resources about the offer.

"Well…" she said, almost apologetically, "I was really hoping for a starting salary of $60,000." Then she said nothing more, allowing the silent pause to hang long enough for the HR manager to think about it and formulate a response.

According to researcher and Carnegie Mellon University professor Linda Babcock, author of *Women Don't Ask*, men are four times more likely than women to initiate negotiations, and women are "much more pessimistic about how much is available when they negotiate." As a result, we tend to ask for less, and, on average, get about 30 percent less than men when we negotiate. So when it comes to income, we start at lower salaries and then continue the trend of avoiding negotiations throughout our careers. Over time, this adds up considerably. "By not negotiating a first salary, an individual stands to lose more than $500,000 by age 60," Dr. Babcock explains. Some studies say the lifetime earning losses are twice that amount—closer to $1 million.

Meg pushed through her discomfort to speak up and ask. She knew the truth of Luke 10:7: "The worker deserves his wages." Even though her stomach was doing flips as the words nervously came out of her mouth, she asked. And you know what? She got it. Lori's starting salary was 32 percent higher than the average starting salary for business majors nationwide during her graduation year. And if her accolades during her first year are any indication, she earned it. Her career is off to a great start, in large part because she aimed high.

If you are already a great negotiator, maybe this topic will be a reminder for you. But if you are like most women, who never ask for more, who cringe at the very idea of negotiating for a better deal, this is for you.

- "I was hoping for X. How close can you get to that number?"

- "I'd like to come to an arrangement we can both feel good about, and right now, this doesn't work for me. Here's what could work: (Describe what you want, be it a higher salary, more vacation time, or a new work-from-home arrangement.) Can we do that?"

- "What would it take for you to _____?"

Once you've asked the question, stop talking. Don't say anything else. When a conversation is uncomfortable, it can be tempting to "stack questions." That's when you ask a question and then immediately stack another question on top of it before giving the person a chance to answer. Sometimes we do it because we want to reword a question we've asked. At other times, we do it because we are anxious or uncomfortable with the boldness of the question we just asked and are afraid of the response we might hear. So we ask another question immediately to soften the effect of the bold question. Resist this temptation. When you ask a bold question, it often requires extra time for the other person to answer. Give the person time. Let the butterflies flutter. Take a breath. Make the decision to wait.

Do you hold yourself back because you think you're not ready, even though coworkers or friends would describe you as ready? Do you avoid negotiation because it makes you super uncomfortable? Do you agonize in meetings about whether or not to share an idea out of fear of having the idea batted down?

Journalists Claire Shipman and Katty Kay say this in a 2014 article for the *Atlantic:* "There is a particular crisis for women—a vast confidence gap that separates the sexes. Compared with men, women don't consider themselves as ready for promotions, they predict they'll do worse on tests, and they generally underestimate their abilities. This disparity stems from factors ranging from upbringing to biology."[1]

Make the decision to speak up more. Make the decision to *try*. Decide that it is okay to say it clumsily, as long as you say it. Give yourself permission to be seen and heard, not because you are perfect but because you are probably better than you think you are. Putting yourself out there will give you a chance to be considered for opportunities—whether personal or professional.

Your Script for Success

- Get clear about what you want. Then open your mouth and ask for it.

- Be willing to accept that you may not get what you want. "No" gives clarity. It gives direction. It can also open the conversation to a modified "yes."

- When you ask for what you want, don't allow nervous energy to cause you to apologize for asking or to undo your original request.

Every Woman Should Know

- When you underestimate your value, you are more likely to expect less from others—and therefore, ask for less. Asking for what you're worth only works when you accurately perceive your worth.

- People use cues you give to quickly determine key information about you. Use this to your advantage. Be intentional about what you communicate through your actions, appearance, and speech.

- Boundaries are your personal decisions about what is okay and what isn't.

Coach Yourself

- What is it that you want that you've been afraid to ask for? Write a script of exactly what you want to say and to whom, and determine a time to ask it. Tell someone of your plan and ask that person to hold you accountable.

- Consider your relationships, your work, and your finances. In what way(s) have you underestimated your value? What changes would be needed in order to more accurately reflect your value and worth?

- How do you feel when you are told "no" to a request that is important to you? In what way(s) have you allowed rejection from your past to keep you from asking for what you want today? What are you willing to do differently in the future?

Speak Differently

The most successful women are not fearless. They are courageous. One of the most powerful signs of courage is your ability to ask for what you want.

Know What Not to Say

*Your words are currency—be careful
how you spend them.*

Even fools are thought wise if they keep silent,
and discerning if they hold their tongues.
PROVERBS 17:28

Key Lessons

- Don't complain if you're not willing to confront.
- You can never take back words said imprudently or in anger.
- You take great personal and professional risk by sending sloppy or overemotional electronic communication.

To teach a lesson, the sixteenth-century priest St. Philip Neri gave an assignment as penance to a woman who had been spreading gossip. He told her to go to the top of the church bell tower with a feather pillow and tear it open, allowing the feathers to be blown away by the wind. She did so and returned to the saint, not sure of the point of the assignment. But he had a second assignment in mind. "Now," he explained when she was done, "go into the streets and fields and collect up all of the feathers that are scattered throughout the town." This, of course, was a task she could never complete.

That was the point of the lesson. Your words, once said, cannot be unsaid. Whether gossip about a coworker or a friend, whether words spewed in a moment of anger or a confidence you reveal that was not yours to share, once released, the words you utter cannot be sealed back up. You might be forgiven for them. But words can change the dynamic of relationships or even create an unfair emotional burden for the people who've heard them.

Consider sisters Liz and Yvonne. Liz was on the verge of leaving her husband of seven years. She'd had enough. And this time, she had a sense of courage and urgency she'd never felt in years past when his behavior became out of control. Liz always complained that he'd "stepped over the line"—she'd probably said that 50 times over the years. But no one was quite sure why Liz called it a "line" because there were never any serious consequences. The only consequence he suffered seemed to be Liz's ranting and yelling.

This time, though, he'd secretly gone into the college savings accounts they'd set up for their children and used the money to day-trade a stock he'd thought would skyrocket quickly. He was trying to make up for the money he'd lost pulling the same silly risks with their retirement accounts. Instead of skyrocketing, the stock tanked and now the kids' accounts had lost 80 percent of their value.

"He didn't even tell me about it," Liz cried into the phone as her sister Yvonne listened. "I found out when I intercepted the mail and opened up the statement. I thought it must be an error when I saw the balance! How can I continue to live like this? He lies. He gambles everything away. It's like living with a spoiled child who is used to someone else cleaning up his mistakes all the time. And he has no real remorse. The more I work to try to make up for his recklessness, the more of a hole he digs. Do you know Mom and Dad let us borrow money to pay off the debt last time he got us into trouble like this? We haven't even finished paying them back and now this! I feel so taken for granted."

Yvonne didn't know about that. She said nothing, but inwardly she had a ping of resentment. *Mom and Dad bailed out you and your husband?* she thought. *You have a solid, two-income household, and you're borrowing money from our retired parents. I have one average income, and I don't ask them for money.* Yvonne couldn't believe her ears, but she wouldn't dare say anything. *Stop being judgmental,* she berated herself. *Your sister's marriage is struggling. Stop thinking about yourself.*

"Have you discussed your concerns with him?" Yvonne asked.

"He just gets defensive and says I'm insecure," Liz responded.

Yvonne had heard her sister's frustrations before, but she heard something different in her sister's voice this time. A resolve to change the situation. That was new, and Yvonne sensed she should offer to support her sister. "I hate to see my baby sister so miserable. I'm so angry at him for not getting it together. It's just not fair to you, and you're going to have to put your foot down. How can I support you, Liz?"

After some counseling and much prayer, Liz told her sister a few weeks later she wanted to separate and asked if she could stay with her for a few months until she could figure out what to do next. Yvonne got her guest room all prepared so her sister would feel at home during what could be a difficult transition.

Liz's husband thought she was bluffing when she told him she was leaving. Even as she packed up her things, he ignored her. Then, on the day Yvonne and other family members were to show up with a moving van, he realized she was serious and did an about-face. He begged her not to go. Promised to do better. Convinced her to stay. She did. He started helping around the house and being extra sweet.

Liz became ecstatic about the changes. Yvonne didn't feel good about it. She believed it would be short-lived and felt deeply worried for her sister.

While Liz was quick to forgive and had hope for change, Yvonne felt protective of her sister. She was sure her brother-in-law was being manipulative to keep Liz from leaving, and she doubted that he had any intentions of real change.

Problem is, Yvonne was sucked into the matter when her sister decided to share in great detail about her husband's behavior—details Yvonne now struggles to unremember. Liz can do her best to gather up the feathers she released, but she'll never gather them all up. Several years have passed. Liz and her husband remain married—unhappily. Liz is still dealing with the same issues, and as much as Yvonne wants to support her sister, she has put her foot down regarding discussions of her sister's marriage.

"I told her that I don't want to hear any more details and complaining unless she's in some sort of danger or she's going to do something about it. I just get too upset about the drama, and it seems like I care more about her than she cares about herself," Yvonne explained.

Knowing what to speak about and with whom is critical to having thriving relationships. Consider the damage that can be done when you share information with people that will get them emotionally charged. But then you move on from the emotion of the situation while the person upon whom you dumped the details is left to deal with the impact of the words you spoke.

Negative Is More Powerful than Positive

Research in the area of positive emotion by renowned University of North Carolina researcher Dr. Barbara Frederickson shows that negative is more powerful than positive. So consider what that looks like in your relationships. When you harp on the negative, use negative body language, and point out everything you feel someone has done wrong without also noticing and acknowledging what he or she has done right, you create a deficit of positive emotion in your interactions in that relationship. Ultimately, that deficit can make communication more difficult.

Let's say you have a negative experience with someone and begin sharing those experiences with other people. Then your relationship improves. You have a few positive experiences and soon your opinion changes along with the relationship. It will take a lot of undoing for the people who were on the receiving end of your negative characterizations. It will take a lot of undoing for the person who was on the receiving end of that conversation. In some cases, the significance of the negative words might be too weighty to ever overcome. When that happens, shortsighted statements can end up undermining relationships in the long term.

The most successful women understand fully how powerful words are. They understand that their words can change the entire course of a family, a career, or a friendship. So they are slow to speak, especially in serious discussions. They think through the consequences of their words before uttering them. And they understand that in many instances, silence is better than a hasty response. "Even fools are thought wise if they keep silent," Proverbs 17:28 promises. Successful women know that, and they feel no pressure to speak an opinion when they don't have enough information to form a meaningful one.

What to Say and What Not to Say

So how do you know what to say and what not to say? Should you just keep everything to yourself, even when you really need to talk things out and have a sounding board to help you make a major decision? Consider these guidelines.

Not every request, challenge, or statement needs a response. People must earn the right to be in relationship with you. And what is the basis of a relationship? Communication. Disrespectful communication does not always warrant a response. After all, if you demand respect, you answer only to respectful conversation. If the tone changes, you can respond accordingly. This is about setting strong boundaries by treating others respectfully, yet requiring the same in return.

Not everyone is the right sounding board. Choose with care. If Liz had considered how the disturbing details of her husband's behavior would affect her sister, she might have decided to speak to a counselor or neutral confidant who wasn't a relative. Before you vent, consider whether or not the information you want to share will affect the person who is your sounding board and the person about whom you are venting. Your children (even your adult children) shouldn't hear you vent about their other parent. Your coworker may feel caught in the middle when you vent about someone they also must work with.

This doesn't mean you can never share pertinent information, but take care before you share details that will shift the dynamics of other relationships. This is especially true in close personal relationships. Even though you may get over the frustration you were venting about, the person who had to listen to you vent may not be able to move forward quite as easily. You may not be able to gather up all of those wind-blown feathers.

Don't let the pressure to be first cause you to speak too soon. In our quest to keep up, to be heard, to be right—it can be easy to speak too soon in a situation. Refuse to succumb to the pressure to chime in too quickly. Once you've stated certain opinions and evaluations, it can be hard to undo them without sounding wishy-washy. Just keep in mind that your words have power and therefore are worthy of thoughtfulness when there is uncertainty. There is a balance, of course. You don't want to be afraid to speak up. But when you don't have a sense of peace committing to a course of action or sharing an opinion, don't speak.

Don't stoke negative emotions unnecessarily. One of my favorite bits of wisdom comes from the book of James. It says this:

> When we put bits into the mouths of horses to make them obey us, we can turn the whole animal. Or take ships as an example. Although they are so large and are driven by strong winds, they are steered by a very small rudder wherever the pilot wants to go. Likewise, the tongue is a small part of the body, but it makes great boasts. Consider what a great forest is set on fire by a small spark (James 3:3-5).

Your words can spark anger, resentment, jealousy, anxiety, fear, anticipation, and many other emotions. Be cognizant of the power of your words on the emotions of others. What will the impact be on those to whom you are speaking? Will the situation resolve itself quickly, and will their emotions be spent in vain? Or is the negative emotion an unavoidable and appropriate element of the situation? Sometimes difficult things must be shared, but drama is usually optional. Remain calm and steady. There is power in calmness.

Speak what you know. Go easy on what you don't. Another time to speak less or not at all is when the subject matter is simply not your area of experience. Don't wing it. Depending on the situation, you can just listen. Or if a question is asked of you, admit what you don't know. When the situation calls for it, offer to find the answer and share it later. If you don't have something meaningful to contribute, resist the urge to talk for the sake of talking. A confident woman speaks because she knows what she has to say adds value to the conversation.

Don't complain if you are not willing to confront. Complaining without a willingness to address solutions is disempowering. Sometimes confronting an issue means talking to the person responsible and asking for a change or correction of some sort. Sometimes it means confronting a problem by seeking a way to change your circumstances. For example, the problem may not be your boss but the career path you've chosen—a much bigger issue. Are you willing to confront it? If not, then make a decision to stop complaining about it.

It might take a while, but you'll find that once you begin taking steps to resolve your problems, you will feel more powerful and purposeful in your life.

> ### Speak kindness.
>
> "Pleasant words are like a honeycomb, sweetness to the soul and health to the bones," Proverbs 16:24 (NKJV) says. Make it your goal to speak words that uplift and encourage whenever possible. Such words strengthen the bonds of relationships, build positive emotion that makes it easier to have difficult conversations later, and generally make you a more pleasant person to spend time with. Find reasons to compliment others, show gratitude, and speak well of others behind their backs.

When to Remain Silent

There are times when it's best to stay quiet—times when your words could only affect the situation negatively. Here are a few times when you should choose not to speak.

When the conversation is foolish. If the person with whom you are conversing is foolish, speaking nonsense, and attempting to engage you in conversation that will require you to stoop down to a level of ignorance, do not engage. Ease out of the conversation, decline to comment, or walk away. Anything you attempt to say in such a situation will likely only escalate the conversation.

When the other person needs your listening ear. One of the most challenging skills for new coaches is silence. We often tell coaches to get comfortable with silence. Give the other person a chance to think, the space to explore their options. Don't try to give them the answers. Allow them to discover their own answers with you as a sounding board and guide. The same holds true in many other conversations. Be cognizant of how much you talk. Do you dominate the conversation? Does the other person feel heard? Being quiet gives the other person the space to enjoy a true back-and-forth conversation with you.

When the moment calls for comfort and sacred listening. Another time that calls for silence is when emotion is involved. Whether a devastating loss or other event a person is still processing, your presence will often be more important than your words. Rather than attempt to give answers or advice, just be there.

Not Everyone Deserves Your Words or Energy

Have you ever found yourself with the perfect comeback for someone, but circumstances precluded you from the perfect opportunity to utter it? In your mind, you have a well-thought-out lecture that person needs to hear. I mean, if they could just get your eye-opening revelations, they could finally get it together! But the more you think about it, the more you realize your words will be nothing more than wasted breath—and maybe the spark for more drama. Sometimes, you must come to the realization that getting others to fix themselves is *not* your responsibility.

It may sound harsh, but not all life lessons are about positivity. Some are about preservation. Your energy is powerful. Don't give it away too easily. Recognize its value and spend it on people and things that give you a return on your investment. If you give it away to people who do not deserve it, you'll waste this precious resource and wonder why you don't have enough energy for the people and things you say matter most. When a situation deserves your energy, you'll notice at least one of these things:

- You are energized by engaging with the person, group, or situation.

- Even if you cannot see the outcome today, you know your energy is being spent on a worthwhile endeavor.

- Your words and energy are moving you toward a solution, not fruitless debate or new problems.

- You feel divinely led to spend your energy there. It is purposeful.

I'm one of those people who gives more chances than I should, but when I'm done, *I'm really done.* I move on, knowing there is nothing more I could have done. I have no guilt. I don't have to second-guess myself. And typically, I get confirmation that my decision was the right one. This is because people who push your boundaries don't stop being who they are just because you wise up. Be discerning about who and what gets your energy. Sometimes, silence is your answer. Preserve your words and energy. Direct them only toward that which is fruitful. Invest your energy in what you want, not what you don't want. Be discerning about who and what deserves a response and what doesn't.

> Consider your own life and circumstances. What situation or person entices you to move into a negative energy state? What would it look like to drop the issue and move on? What deserves your positive energy instead?

Speaking of People

Stephanie was frustrated with a friend and trying to figure out how to approach the situation. She hesitantly broached the subject with Tia, a mutual friend, hoping that perhaps Tia could listen and brainstorm with her about what to say.

"I really don't want to talk behind her back, but I need some advice. I don't want to lose her friendship, but I also feel if I don't say something, that's what's going to happen anyway," Stephanie agonized.

Tia could feel a bit of a knot forming in the pit of her stomach. She loved both women and didn't want to be disloyal to either. She could tell Stephanie really needed some advice, though, and her attitude about it was sincere, not jaded or angry. And that's when Tia remembered something that is a great rule of thumb. The Bible is clear about two things when it comes to talking about others: Neither gossip nor flattery is acceptable. I like to remember it this way:

Gossip is saying something about someone behind her back that you wouldn't say to her face.

Flattery is saying something to someone's face that you wouldn't say behind their back.

Remembering those definitions, Tia was loving but straightforward with Stephanie. "You seem really conflicted. You know I love you both, so I want to help if I can, but here's the thing," she said sweetly but directly. "Whatever you tell me, be willing to tell her too. I don't want to gossip about her, but I do want to help." Stephanie agreed and told Tia her dilemma.

Tia's advice included suggesting Stephanie write down the three things she most needed to say or ask of their friend. And Tia asked Stephanie to preface the conversation with this: "I have been so anxious about talking to you about this. I wasn't sure if I should say anything, so I asked Tia's advice because she knows us both. She said I should just talk to you about it because you'd listen."

No gossip. Everything out in the open. And clear boundaries set up front. If success is a harmony of purpose, resilience, and joy—especially in our relationships—then you must speak with integrity about people. It can be easy to get caught up in gossip, whether at work, among friends, or in the community, but true success means never reveling in someone else's problems or stirring up seeds of discord. In some crowds, that means you'll stand out. But that's what you're meant to do. You speak differently. You use your words to uplift, build, and strengthen.

Speaking of people, flattery is just as damaging. Those who flatter others by saying things they don't believe in order to gain favor with them are eventually found out. Authenticity is a hallmark of resilience. Resilience is a hallmark of success. With practice, it is possible to find the good in others that you can authentically compliment without resorting to flattery. And if you resort to simply saying to others what they want to hear, even the most insecure people know the difference between real compliments and fake ones.

Gossiping is saying something about someone behind their back that you wouldn't say to their face. Flattery is saying something to someone's face that you wouldn't say behind their back.

Speaking with Your Keyboard

One woman was traveling from New York to South Africa to see family for the holidays and amusing herself by tweeting thoughts along the way. Her job title at the time was senior director of corporate communications for a major online media company. About her flight from New York to London, she tweeted about a "weird German dude" who needed deodorant. While waiting for her connecting flight from London to Cape Town, she tweeted about "bad teeth" in London. And then just before takeoff, she tweeted this: "Going to Africa. Hope I don't get AIDS. Just kidding. I'm white!"

According to a recount of the trip in the *New York Times Magazine*, the woman "chuckled as she pressed send on this last one," and then wandered the airport for a while before her flight. She checked her phone, but no one responded to her tweet. With fewer than 200 followers, it wasn't unusual. She made her flight and slept most of the way on the eleven-hour flight to South Africa. Upon landing, she turned on her phone and immediately knew something was wrong. An old high school friend had texted an "I'm sorry" message. Another friend had asked her to call right away. Then she got a call saying she was the number-one worldwide trend on Twitter.

During her eleven-hour flight her "joke" had set off a firestorm on Twitter with tens of thousands angry replies and calls for her to be fired (even by employees at her company who caught wind of the tweet). In fact, someone on Twitter in South Africa went to the airport just to get a picture of her arrival and posted it online. Even though her best friend managed to get into her account and delete the tweet and her Twitter account while she was still flying, it was too late.

The woman acknowledged that she never should have made the AIDS comment. She believed it was so ridiculous of a comment that no one would actually believe she meant it. She wrote to the *New York Times Magazine*, "I had no business commenting on an epidemic in such a politically incorrect manner on a public platform. To put it simply, I wasn't trying to raise awareness of AIDS…or ruin my life. Living in America puts us in a bubble when it comes to what is going on in the third world. I was making fun of that bubble."[1]

I do not understand the rationale or sense of humor that led her to post what she posted, but I do believe her that she wasn't intending to ruin her life when she posted it. She lost her job. She brought grief on her family in South Africa, who had been activists for racial equality there. And her name will forever be tied to that tweet anytime someone searches her online.

Social Media

The "feather effect" from the beginning of this chapter can be just as dramatic, if not more so, when you speak from your keyboard. Unlike speaking one-on-one or even to a finite number of people, speaking from your social media platforms creates a permanent record and the opportunity to grow exponentially as others share what you post. Many people treat the very public platform of social media as though it were a cozy, private chat with friends in a living room. It's not. You can say something indiscriminate to a family member or friend and correct yourself. You can show remorse and ask forgiveness. And you'll probably be able to move on from it. You might even argue with them, but the content of what you said cannot be easily shared with the entire world, your employer, your neighbor, and every friend you had in high school. Do not treat a public platform like a private conversation. It is safest to just cut out tacky jokes altogether, but at the very least, don't post them for the world to see.

This is bigger, however, than offensive jokes. Unlike the last century, today just about everyone has a public persona. I'm sure you do. You probably have multiple social media accounts. Here's what successful women do on social media: They remember their vision and their goals, and they ensure that anything they post on social media is aligned with how they want to show up in the world. They do not post anything that could sabotage their best efforts—whether a career or business goal, relationship goal, financial or spiritual goal. They don't forget that it isn't just their personal friends reading their posts but everyone they've connected with online—whether coworkers, customers, potential employers, neighbors, in-laws, fellow church members, or nieces and nephews. Keep that in mind when you post. If your posts were ever to go viral, they could be exposed to millions of people with whom you have no connection whatsoever.

Today, individuals are comfortable sharing their innermost thoughts in the comment sections of articles and posts. Remember, those comments can be seen by people you don't know. People can see information about your profile with just the click of a button. People have been fired for writing offensive comments, forgetting that they've listed their employer under their full name on their own page. Angry commenters have been known to screenshot comments and contact employers. Be intentional about what you say anywhere online. If you must comment, comment in line with your vision and goals. Make it something that shifts the conversation in a productive direction.

Whatever social media you most enjoy engaging, ask yourself this question: What is my purpose for sharing on this social media platform? If you understand your purpose for using a particular social media site, that purpose can guide your approach to it. Is it to stay abreast of what friends and family are up to? Follow certain people for inspiration or information? Position you as a subject-matter expert? Share photos with family and friends?

When you know your reason for being on a particular platform, it becomes easy to decide what you want to convey from your platform. This one question, "What is the purpose of me being on this social media platform?" is powerful. You might even decide, after answering the question, that you no longer want to be part of some platforms.

They hold no real purpose for you. For other platforms, you will suddenly see clearly what you should post and what you shouldn't.

For example, on my Facebook page, my mission is to inspire fans with practical daily insights and help them get to know me better. Most of what I post is inspiration, but it is sprinkled with personal posts that are fun and positive or meaningful. I realize my brand is about successful women, and whatever I post needs to be relevant for them. Even if I post about my husband or children or parents or friends, it is in the context of something women who care about success can relate to—because ultimately, I'm on Facebook to connect with you, my reader.

Email Conveys No Emotion

Once you press send on that email, it's out there—in writing. And because it is so tough to convey tone and emotion via email, it is risky to send messages that are emotional or may evoke emotion.

If you need to convey more than just key information, have a verbal conversation. You can share foundational information via email, when appropriate, and then follow up with a face-to-face or phone conversation to discuss the rest.

If you are upset about something, do not send an email. Wait until you feel calm. Take time to think through what you want to say. With every statement you feel compelled to make, ask yourself, "Does this statement move me closer to my goal for this communication?" If so, keep moving forward. If not, eliminate the statement or adjust it to meet your goal. Be purposeful about your communication, and that means taking care not to release feathers you'll later want to recover but can't.

Of course, email is not the only way to speak from your keyboard. For many positions today, a company will run not only a criminal background check and credit report on potential employees, but a social media background check as well. That includes anything you've posted or that has been posted about you on social media, blogs, search engines, and anywhere else online. These social media background checks, which the Federal Trade Commission deemed lawful and within compliance of the Fair Credit Reporting Act (FCRA), can go back up to seven years to report what you've said, what's been said about you, and any photographs or videos you've posted. If such a check was run on you today, what would it reveal about how you speak and what you present to the world? Would it reflect the image and values that best represent you?

We communicate with the written word more than ever before. And it can impact how people see you. Is your writing style hypercasual, punctuation optional, and random auto-corrected? How do you imagine that might influence other people's perception of you?

Permanent Trail

Speaking of electronic communication, the illustration of St. Philip Neri and the woman who spread gossip is even more relevant in this age of technology. Just as it was impossible for the woman to gather up all of the feathers once released, it is impossible to recant statements and comments made through electronic communication. While it has become our norm to communicate via text and email, spout off opinions in the comment sections of social media, or share pictures and videos through electronic media, be intentional about creating your own rules for using technology to communicate.

Take a moment now to think about it. It is so easy to simply do what everybody else is doing, but you aren't "everybody else." You are a woman of purpose, resilience, and joy. That means you're intentional about how and what you communicate, understanding that once released, you can't undo certain communication. You can apologize. You can try to make up for it. You can inform someone that you have changed your mind and no longer feel that way. You can make excuses. But you cannot cause someone to unread what you've written or "unhear" what you've said.

All sorts of unnecessary drama occurs because of a casual attitude toward electronic communication. It can become a source of confusion and chaos unless you take seriously the consequences of careless communication. One of the keys to avoiding regret is to decide in advance what your own personal rules are when it comes to texting, email, voice mail, social media, audio recordings, and videos. Here are a few categories in which you can intentionally set your own rules. Consider these categories and questions to identify your own standards now so that you don't have to make spur-of-the-moment rules when faced with a tempting scenario:

Texting

Texting is an efficient and casual way to communicate. What are your rules about when, what, and whom to text—or not text? These rules will be specific to you, but I'll share some examples. I generally text friends and family but not people who are clients or vendors. I try to stick to email for professional communication unless I'm in the midst of an engagement for the client and we need to communicate in real time.

What's my reason for this? Typically, the message isn't that urgent, and they can't save and file texts the way one can organize an email. And texting has a sense of urgency to it that can cause unnecessary stress when you're working. Overall, your personal rules about texting don't need to include a list of what *to* text, but it can be wise to make a decision about what you will *not* text. This might include paragraphs of information, questions that require detailed explanation, or information that would be upsetting or shocking to get via text, which, as noted, is a casual form of communication.

Also, make a decision not to text anything you wouldn't want someone else to read. Whether it is a photo you don't want forwarded or a statement that could get you into hot water if someone else were to read it, think before you text. Your text might be casual, but it is also a time-stamped and dated statement. Ask yourself this question: If the person to whom I am sending this text showed it to someone else, would I be embarrassed, angry, or hurt by it in some way? If the answer is yes, don't send it. Think for a moment about some of the personal rules you would like to set for texting and jot them down. What are your standards?

Email

Unlike texting, email can be a formal mode of communication. And because emails are often kept for years, whatever you speak via email should be intentional. Set some basic rules for how you approach email. For example, you could decide to respond to work emails that are serious in nature only when you are in work mode. By "serious in nature," I mean emails that require a thoughtful response, have consequences beyond answering a simple question, or evoke emotion within you. Particularly when an email causes you to feel emotional, refuse to answer it immediately after you read it. Give yourself time to process what you've read and reply with a message that is intentional and non-emotional. Here's a general rule of thumb:

- Regroup before replying to emotion-provoking emails. Take a break, walk away—even sleep on it when appropriate.

- Rather than make accusations, stick with facts. Ask direct questions so you can get clarity rather than make assumptions.

- Remember that emotion and nuances are often lost via email. Therefore, if something must be said that conveys emotion, it is often better to pick up the phone or talk face-to-face. However, if you need to communicate in written form to protect yourself or document the conversation, do your best to convey nuances and emotionally relevant information by stating them.

- Use bullet points to convey important points so that key information is easy to access and long emails do not become overwhelming.

- If you need a specific reply, ask for it more than once and specifically ask for it at the end of the email since it will be the last thing the recipient reads.

Voice Mail

With so many modes of electronic communication, voice mail has, in some ways, become subject to a generational gap—especially for personal communication. The older you are, the more likely you are to leave voice mail—and the longer the messages you are willing to leave. Millennials often report they consider voice mail impractical and don't consider the messages particularly urgent because if they are, why not send a text? Plus, a voice mail message takes longer to retrieve and process than a text. If you use voice mail in the workplace, however, remember a couple of things when leaving messages:

- Unless a message is about subject matter that is negative or disappointing in some way, smile while you are leaving the message. It makes you sound more energetic and engaging.

- Keep the message short and to the point. Answer who, what, when, where, and why.

- Never leave a message when you are not in a fully present mental state. Don't multitask and leave a message. And certainly don't leave messages while you are emotional. Just like all electronic communication, voice mail can be saved, forwarded, and used against you later.

A good rule of thumb is to leave only informational or positive messages via voice mail unless the information cannot be conveyed in any other way. When there is something to say that will negatively impact the recipient, leaving a voice message means they can listen to it repeatedly, share with other people, and dissect your message in ways they could not if they had an actual conversation with you. Your words have impact. If you record your words, make sure the message is one you wouldn't mind being replayed.

Video

No medium is more powerful than video. And today, video is easier to shoot and disseminate than ever before—and at a high quality. The visual of your movement and the sound of your voice create an image that is unforgettable and impactful. Just remember that whatever you share, whether via text or on social media or anywhere else, is like those feathers in the wind once it is out of your hands. Is it the message you'd want everyone to see? Does it move you closer to your goals or further away from them? Will it attract the kind of attention you want or repel it? Be intentional.

Your Script for Success

- Successful women don't gossip. If you have an issue with someone, be authentic and address it with them. If a person has an issue that does not concern you, keep your judgments to yourself.
- Do not write anything online—whether email, text, or social media—that you do not want kept as a record.
- Speaking differently sometimes means not speaking at all. Remember that not everything deserves a response.

Every Woman Should Know

- Once uttered, your words cannot be "unsaid." Be slow to speak and quick to listen.
- Negative is more powerful than positive. It will take at least three positives to undo a negative.
- Gossip is cowardice—saying something behind someone's back you wouldn't say to his or her face.

Coach Yourself

- When you need to respond to a situation, ask yourself, "Am I overly emotional right now? How much time do I need to give myself to calm down and respond rationally?"

If you don't have time to get centered, ask, "What would be the most spiritually and emotionally mature response right now?"

- What is the purpose of your social media platform? Who is your audience, and what do you want your followers and friends to feel and think when they see your posts?

- When are you most likely to gossip? Whom do you gossip about and why? Whom do you tend to flatter and why? What will you change in order to eliminate gossip and flattery from your speaking habits?

Speak Differently

Silence speaks volumes. Speak with purpose by not speaking at every opportunity. Your words will have more weight.

Don't Just Speak Positively— Speak Accurately

Why you need the courage to replace excuses with the truth—right now.

Then you will know the truth, and the truth will set you free.
JOHN 8:32

Key Lessons

- Though it may be difficult to hear, the truth reveals your opportunity for growth and breakthrough.
- Staying positive all the time is not a requirement for success.
- Once you own a problem, you can take the responsibility to resolve it.

I turned the key in the ignition and switched the heat to high. It was a cold autumn day, and this conversation was going to take a while. And even if it didn't, getting myself together enough to walk back into the building and past my employees to get to my office would take a minute.

As the tears streamed down my face, my mother assured me supportively, "Maybe it's time to do something else. You just seem so stressed and so unhappy in this business." Her words rang true, but I was afraid to admit it. What on earth was I supposed to do with that truth? I started the business. I marketed it. I hired people—not just any people, actually. Some were people I knew and cared about before I even hired them. And now I wanted to pursue something new.

That was the truth. But I had never actually said it out loud before. I was scared to, but even at 28, the safe space of my mother's gentle nudge lowered the wall of fear that kept the truth at bay.

The day had started with a request for a proposal for new business. Such news excites most business owners, but it had caused a tightness in my chest. I didn't enjoy the work, and frankly, I didn't really want any more of it. That felt like a pretty ridiculous thing to admit as a business owner. But it was the news that afternoon that had caused me to rush out of the office before anyone could get a glimpse of the tears that were kind enough to wait until I made it out of the building and into the driver's seat of my car before they began to stream down my cheeks.

It was around the time of the dot-com bust. A client—not my biggest client, but an easy and consistent client—had called to tell me they were losing business and had to cut back on expenses. They would need to cut their public relations budget. At the sound of this news, my heart sank. Using my most professional voice, I was sympathetic and understanding, but I had to get off the phone quickly before the facade cracked. I didn't want any new clients, but I didn't want to lose the ones we had either. I wanted status quo while I figured out how to make a transition to the career that was calling me. Sometimes, though, I think we take too long, and God hurries us along by forcing us to stare fear in the face.

"Mom, the truth is, I don't want to do this anymore, but I'm scared," I admitted.

"You don't *have* to run this business," she said matter-of-factly. "You chose to start it, and you can choose to move on from it." I sat with the words for a moment, sniffling every couple of seconds as I wiped my face. I took a deep breath and allowed her words to sink in. I didn't know how to move on, but in that moment I knew that moving on was the right answer.

There is immense power in speaking the truth. It wants to come out. It wants to be acknowledged. And once you speak it, that power gains a life of its own. "Life and death are in the power of the tongue," Proverbs 18:21 (NKJV) promises. Whether we speak the truth or we deny it, we can literally create the direction of our lives by the words that come out of our mouths—or the words that don't. If I had denied the truth that day, I would have killed the divine plan that was waiting to unfold. I could have continued pretending all was well. And doing so would have given life to a lie.

So much was going right in my public relations business at the time, but there was this one underlying problem—I had finally discovered my life's work, and it wasn't public relations. That pesky little truth meant I was in the wrong business, and no amount of success at it was going to change that problem. The change that needed to happen would only happen with the courage to acknowledge the truth.

Have you ever been in that position? Whether in a relationship or a career or with your finances or health, the truth reveals your opportunity for growth and breakthrough.

You Know You're in Self-Defense Mode When...

Pam gets really stressed every time a project deadline nears. Her boss says she needs to work on lowering her anxiety because her attitude is negatively impacting the team members who report to her. This feedback aggravates Pam and only increases her stress.

Gina has listened to her husband complain for months about her social media habits. He calls it an addiction, which was just completely over the top in her opinion. "I love staying connected with my friends, especially now that we've moved away," she explains. "And lulling out on social media helps me unwind."

Cameron's goal of making the leap from employee to small business owner has hit a lot of snags. She's had her public relations consulting side gig for four years and thought surely she'd be completely solo by now, but the clients she's attracting don't seem to have big enough budgets to justify leaving her full-time job just yet. A friend of hers who owns a successful graphic design business noted that Cameron is targeting individuals rather than corporate entities with real marketing budgets—an audience that will likely never get her to her goal. But the different approach her friend suggested would take Cameron out of her comfort zone, so she dismisses it.

Perhaps you, like each of these women, have received feedback from people that didn't sit well with you. Maybe it made you uncomfortable or caused you to feel criticized when you were working hard to do things right. But deep down, if you are truly honest, you realize the feedback isn't totally off base. If you ever find that little, tiny voice of reason in those quiet moments pondering a dilemma, saying, *"You know, she's not all wrong. You do that sometimes, and it's kind of a problem,"* and then you toss the thought aside quickly because of what it would mean to acknowledge it, consider this: You are silencing the voice that could be the saving grace of what really, really matters to you.

Many goals are sabotaged by the defensive instincts of self-preservation. "I can't admit my faults or I'll lose." Lose what? you might ask. Lose the argument. Lose the opportunity. Lose the right to keep behaving the way you do. Lose your comfort zone. You might not say, "I can't admit I'm wrong or I'll lose" out loud, but at a visceral level, that's what you are saying.

Perhaps you've had the experience in the past of admitting a mistake and getting beat up for it. Maybe that unintentional error got you fired or cost you the promotion. Perhaps you admitted you were wrong in an effort to be truthful in a relationship in hopes of building trust, but instead the other person never let you live it down and still brings it up to this day. Wherever you first formed the habit of preemptive self-defense as a means of preserving your standing, it is a habit that can hold you back in a major way.

This can be a really uncomfortable topic. If you are sensitive to feedback and see it as criticism, then my giving you feedback right now about how you receive feedback might feel like a double whammy! So take a deep breath. Close your eyes for just a moment and recall the reason you felt compelled to pick up this book in the first place. You want something, and you believe you'll gain some knowledge that can help you get there. Perhaps you liked the idea of gaining more courage or confidence or influence in your life. This is your invitation to be courageous.

One of the most important decisions successful women make is that they actively seek feedback and use it to grow. It would be so lovely if feedback was always just what our ears wanted to hear. I love hearing what I do well. It is important to hear that because if you know what you do well, you can be intentional about repeating that behavior. Such feedback builds on your strengths and can feel very affirming and motivating. But receiving feedback about what you should consider changing requires a level of emotional and spiritual honesty that many of us refuse to have. I am not talking about spurious criticisms here. I am talking about legitimate concerns.

Here's how it looks when you reject feedback that feels hard to hear but could propel you forward if you embraced it:

- You get angry at the person who gives you the feedback, even if he or she says it in a kind way.

- You make excuses for the mistake, fault, or error that was pointed out.

- You brush it off even though you would give the same feedback if the roles were reversed.

- You deny the feedback is even accurate.

- You avoid the person in the future because you don't want to address the issue.

- You point out the flaws of the person giving the feedback. "How dare they point out my flaws when they have their own?"

- You gather up evidence of others who do not agree with the assessment (even when you sense in your spirit that the assessment is valid).

- You try to put the feedback out of your mind.

When you get feedback that is difficult to hear but might actually have validity, what keeps you from receiving it? Here are a few common culprits:

- The messenger is flawed and you don't want to hear the message from that person.

- You are afraid of the consequences of acknowledging the problem.
- You are afraid to address the issue.
- You don't know what to do about it.
- You feel shame, embarrassment, or guilt about it.

Replacing Truth with Excuses

When you operate out of emotions such as fear, blame, shame, embarrassment, or guilt, the pain feels very real. Your first reaction can be to flinch just as you do when the pain is physical. It is self-preservation to want to escape the pain or protect yourself from it. The same happens on an emotional level, and it tends to come out in your reaction through the words you speak. You can gloss over it by minimizing the perceived fault. You can deny it is even true. You can attack the messenger by pointing out how he or she has no authority and credibility to talk about your flaws given his or her own. Or you can make excuses for it.

For example, Pam's response to her boss's critique was to point out that "the deadlines were too intense for me to act happy." In other words, the deadlines were an excuse to act out. This isn't to say the stress didn't impact Pam's reactions, but stress does not excuse yelling or belittling your team members' efforts, which Pam had in fact done.

Gina responded to her husband's complaint about her social media habit by insisting she wasn't on her phone "all that much." In truth, during the week before he brought up the subject with her, she checked her phone every single night in bed before they went to sleep. He felt ignored and unimportant. Gina simply denied it was true because it was only for a few minutes. By the time the few minutes had passed each night, though, her husband had dozed off to sleep.

And Cameron, who feels intimidated about presenting herself in new business settings, insists that she "prefers working with aspiring authors, artists, and musicians," even though her business is in a metro area that doesn't have a large arts scene.

In each case, the words these women spoke were not rooted in truth.

I'm not talking about whether the words were truthfully how they felt. I'm talking about whether the words were excuses to cover up deeper truths about the situation. Their excuses glossed over key facts, shirked responsibility for behavior, or allowed them to proceed as though nothing was wrong.

There is a powerful alternative to excuse-making that the most successful women embrace. It requires standing firmly in the belief that the truth will indeed make you free. The truth will release you to move toward your highest potential. It is scary. It will cause you to see yourself in an unflattering light at times. But in doing so, it will also empower you to see clearly, warts and all, what you are dealing with. And once you know that, you will use your words and energy to address the blocks that hold you back from the true desires of your heart.

I call this powerful alternative "speaking the grain of truth." It means you own your faults. Speak them. Acknowledge them. Shine the light on them. Darkness cannot persist where there is light. You don't even have to know how to fix the problem yet. The first step is to admit there is one and that it deserves your attention, not your denial. Shining light on it isn't just thinking about it. It is *speaking* it. Out loud.

I wonder if right now there is a grain of truth that has been ringing true while you are reading this chapter. Speak it out loud right now. Own it. Admit it. When you own your truth, no matter how frustrating or painful or embarrassing, you diminish its power. When you hide it or deny it, you give it power to shame and guilt you. It controls you. You spend energy ignoring, blaming, and denying when you could spend that same energy acknowledging, repairing, and growing.

Own Your Truth

In my years of studying and teaching resilience, one of the skills that most transformed my life and the lives of clients is the act of speaking the grain of truth. When you come to a life coach or a personal trainer, a self-help book or a success seminar, you generally expect to hear a whole lot of talk about "thinking positively." Now this might be something you love. You may have come out of the womb with a smile on your face and a giggle on your lips. Maybe your first words were "I can do it!" Your positivity might be so infectious it annoys your pessimistic sister or coworker.

Or maybe you struggle to stay positive. You start out toward the goal optimistic, but then you hit a bump and start to doubt yourself. Your words go from "I can do this" to "Why am I bothering to try this?"

Sound familiar? I've been there, and I am a pretty positive person. It takes a lot of intention to stay positive all of the time. But here's the good news: Staying positive all the time is not a requirement for success. It helps to stay positive most of the time, and you want to be sure to lift yourself out of a slump, noticing self-sabotaging thoughts when they begin to take over, but research shows nonstop positivity can actually be a hindrance. If you can understand when positivity is needed and when a dose of pessimism is in your best interest, you can greatly increase your chances for reaching a goal. Let me explain.

Back to Pam, who takes her stress out on her coworkers. Pam is one of the best the company has ever seen when it comes to her technical ability. And she loves receiving praise for her talent. She craves it. It makes her feel appreciated, intelligent, needed, and special.

But Pam operates on what I describe in my book *Successful Women Think Differently* as a fixed mindset. People with a fixed mindset believe that attributes such as talent or intelligence are set, so when challenges come along that threaten to undermine their label as "talented" or "intelligent" or "special" in some way, it can rock their very perception of who they are.

For Pam, any feedback that isn't praise for a job well done feels like an attack on who she is as a person, not just a critique on what she could do differently to improve. This, in part, explains her aggravation at her boss for requesting she improve her communication because of the negative impact it is beginning to have on her team. The truth is if she can learn to speak differently to her team, especially when she feels pressured, she may open huge doors of opportunity to go to the next level. But as it stands now, her talent is terrific, but talent alone will not move her closer to her goal because her communication habits are an albatross. The missing pieces—connection and communication—are what she needs to reach her goals at work. Here's how it would look for Pam to speak the grain of truth:

- "You know, I don't enjoy admitting it, but I'm sure I'm not exactly the most encouraging boss when I get stressed out. Maybe I should think about the impact that has on my team."

- "The fact that I need to improve my communication skills does not erase the many good things I do in terms of productivity. It just means I have room for improvement. We all do."

- "I am afraid if I acknowledge that my boss is right, I am admitting that I do not deserve a promotion. I could look at this another way. Acknowledging the truth in my boss's evaluation empowers me to make the changes that will lead to a promotion."

- "I own the fact that I sometimes allow stress to completely take over my personality. This is an opportunity to take a deep breath, turn over my weaknesses to God, and allow His strength to prevail through me."

- "I can be fearful or I can be courageous. I choose courage. I am afraid that I do not know how to fix this problem, but I am willing to face it because I cannot conquer what I will not confront."

- "This problem is an opportunity in disguise. I will focus on a solution. I will seek feedback on how to resolve it. I will grow as a result. I will be better than ever as a result."

By speaking the grain of truth, Pam acknowledges her fears, but she also speaks to her ability to overcome those fears with courage and faith. She owns the problem, and once she owns it, she can take responsibility to resolve it. She can also address her faulty belief that admitting she is not perfect in her job somehow means that she is not worthy of advancing within the organization. If that were the case, none of us would ever see progress!

Women often wear perfectionism as a badge of honor. But perfectionism is rooted in fear, and it is actually the enemy of progress.

Where Do You Need to Speak the Grain of Truth?

Sometimes it isn't a person that gives feedback. Sometimes it is, as my grandmama would have called it, "the unction of the Holy Spirit." You have a deep inner sense about something that is inconvenient to admit. For the most part, a particular situation is fine, but there is this one piece that is off. That's the grain of truth you need to own. If you can own that one grain of truth enough to speak it, you can begin to ponder a solution.

You may not have a professional issue to deal with like Pam. Perhaps, like Gina, you have a hard time hearing feedback from your spouse. How dare he point out your one flaw when you feel that he has five? Maybe it isn't your spouse but another relationship where someone important is telling you what he or she needs, but you tend to brush it off. It could be a doctor who has asked you to make a lifestyle change, but you insist the problem isn't that serious. You don't need to cut out *all* the fried foods, right? Plus soft drinks? You're just bigger boned than most. That body mass index thing doesn't apply to you the same way because you're built differently.

The list of scenarios the grain of truth applies to is endless. But speaking from personal experience, speaking the grain of truth will completely change your life. It changed mine. More than once.

I know what it feels like to be terrified to admit the truth. I will never forget, in my twenties, racking up what felt like so much debt that I felt as though I had a weight on my neck constantly. When I read Scriptures about money, I felt ashamed. My life didn't reflect their truths. "The borrower is servant to the lender," Proverbs 22:7 (NKJV) says. *Yep, that's right,* I thought. Because everything I was making was already spent—owed to my car lender, student loan company, credit card companies. I wanted to be debt free.

So I did what I've done many times in my life when I wanted to learn about something but didn't know where to start. I bought a book. It was a good book with simple advice. You see, on the most basic level, I knew how to get out of debt. It's kind of like knowing how to lose weight—exercise more, eat healthier. We all know *how*, but that doesn't mean we do it. There's a big difference between knowing and doing. To get out of debt, it helps to bring in more money and spend less of it. Sometimes you don't even have to do both. If you have enough available to pay off the debt, you're good.

The book I purchased started with a very simple request: Add up your debt. I am not exaggerating when I tell you I put the book back up on the shelf and didn't pick it back up for months. I knew my financial picture didn't look the way I wanted it to, but the idea of knowing an exact number terrified me. I didn't want to know. I was in denial.

Then one day, my car needed to be fixed. It was just a few hundred dollars. The problem was, I had not paid myself in three months. I had paid employees and bills in the PR business I had at the time, but some clients were very late with their payments. It added up to quite a sum, so I made up for it by suspending my salary.

To make matters worse, I could no longer remain in denial about my credit card habit because I was so maxed out I didn't have the available credit to pay for the car repair. And I sure didn't want to admit to anyone that I was having money problems. No. That was just too embarrassing.

The whole facade was cracked, but I was still trying to glue the pieces together to make things look good. I didn't want anyone to know my secret—I looked more successful than I actually was. Here I was driving around in a "luxury" car and couldn't even afford a minor repair on it.

My pride wouldn't let me speak the truth until I was so stressed a close friend asked what was going on. I explained, and without hesitation, the friend pulled out a checkbook and started writing a check for $1000. "No, no. I can't take money from you," I insisted, even though I really needed it. My friend would not relent, so I said, "Okay, how about just $500?" I felt relieved and grateful, yet deflated. And deflation, as negative as it might sound, was the emotion I needed.

My circumstances didn't line up with what I wanted to believe about my financial picture—that I was doing just fine. Borrowing money from a friend was a wake-up call. Sure, I could borrow from a credit card company and tell myself everything was under control. But verbalizing my situation—actually speaking it out loud—made me confront reality, the truth. And it was at that point that I realized it was time to pick that book up off the shelf and face my problem. And so began my journey toward financial security.

I spoke the grain of truth and it sounded something like this: "Valorie, you need to get to a better place financially. You don't make enough money for all of the effort and stress you experience in your business. You let companies pay late rather than speaking up by calling them. Your debt is growing and so is your stress level. Something needs to change in your approach to money."

I called my best friend at the time. Although as an educator she made less money than I did, she had no debt and a very healthy savings account. She lived within her means and seemed content financially. I decided I would speak my grain of truth to her. Even though she never would have gotten herself into the predicament I was in, partially because she had no entrepreneurial aspirations and was more risk averse than I, I knew she would not judge me.

I called her up and told her what I told no one else. I told her how embarrassed I was and how stressed. I told her my goal of becoming debt free. Her response? "Valorie, I can only imagine how stressed you are. But I know you. Once you set your mind to something, you'll do it. And I know you will reach your goal."

I shone the light on the grain of truth by sharing it with someone I trusted. Rather than hiding the grain of truth or denying it, it was now out in the open. I believe that one simple act, using my voice to acknowledge the truth, was a powerful step toward dealing with the truth.

I'm not saying this is easy. It's often scary. It's hard. It'll make your stomach turn into knots as you imagine the worst-case scenarios of what might happen if you step into the light of truth. I've been there. Have you had that dream where you suddenly realize you're in a public place with absolutely nothing on? That's how it can feel to speak the grain of truth—your flaws are on display for criticism, your choices are up for scrutiny, and maybe your very judgment will be called into question. And if that happens, then what? Will you just set yourself up for more things to be criticized?

Step One: Admit There's Something You Don't Want to Admit

Your first step is so simple. It isn't to speak the grain of truth but simply to admit there even is a grain of truth to be examined. This is just coming clean, being honest, and ceasing to deny reality. There is a certain amount of relief that comes with this step.

Remember Gina, the woman whose husband called her social media habits an addiction? She didn't like his characterization of her connecting with her friends and unwinding in the evenings one bit. He was always exaggerating, she said. Why couldn't he just say he wanted more of her attention? Did he really have to go *there*? He didn't have to give something she enjoyed such a negative label.

Her reaction was to dig her heels in and tell him he was being ridiculous. But deep down, she was actually bothered by her own compulsion. It felt unhealthy, but she was afraid to admit it. And that was what she needed to admit: the fear.

In a coaching session, I asked Gina what was the worst part of saying out loud that she had an unhealthy compulsion to constantly check her phone. "It feels like weakness," she said. "And I hate to feel weak."

I probed a little further. "What's so terrible about feeling weak? I mean, we all have weaknesses."

She paused for a long moment and gave a sigh. "Well," she explained, "if I'm weak, I'm imperfect. I'm flawed." She stopped for an even longer moment. "I know this sounds crazy, but I feel like if I'm weak and flawed, I'm not lovable."

Wow. So deep down, Gina rejected her husband's complaint because admitting he was right was the equivalent of giving him permission not to love her anymore.

While this might sound like a stretch, the truth is our fears are often a stretch. They are a string of beliefs that cause us to behave in ways that protect us. Our fears are all about self-preservation. By pausing long enough to acknowledge that there is something you're afraid to admit and then asking yourself what's at the root of your fear, you begin the journey toward courage.

Step Two: Shine the Light on It

Your second step is freeing and scary at the same time. Once you give yourself permission to admit there's something to examine, identify examples of how that grain of truth is showing up. How has it impacted you? How has it impacted others? How does it hold you back from your truest desires?

Even for the smallest truth, you can find a lot of examples of its effect. That may sound overwhelming, but actually, it is empowering. You've just identified something that you have the power to address simply by the fact that you are willing to own it.

Gina made the courageous decision to admit the problem. She shone the light on it and actually admitted it wasn't just social media; it was her whole relationship with her phone. "I check for text messages and social media updates at the stoplight," she told me. "I'm checking my phone while I'm walking down the cereal aisle at the grocery store. When I wake up, I want to pray, stretch, throw on some workout clothes, and take a walk, but instead, do you know what I do first thing upon opening my eyes in the morning? *I reach over to the nightstand and grab my phone.* I know it is unhealthy. I need to stop. I waste so much time."

Shining the light on it means speaking it out loud—first, to yourself. I recommend writing it down. Try it now:

I hate to admit it, but

Some of the ways this is showing up in my life and/or work right now are

This issue has sabotaged my best intentions by

The fact that I am admitting this grain of truth does not negate my positive actions and character traits and many things I do well, such as

However, my potential will be limited until I address the grain of truth. And so, I choose to speak the grain of truth.

Once you've spoken the grain of truth to yourself, speak it to someone you trust. You don't have to discuss it with the person(s) you impact with this grain of truth just yet. That comes next.

Step Three: Leverage the Grain of Truth to Move Forward

It's time to focus on the solution, not the problem. Denial and blame are fear based. When you mature emotionally and spiritually, you realize the power of telling the truth to yourself and others.

Let go of what you think people will think. Refuse to beat yourself up. Give yourself permission to be imperfect. And recognize that by speaking the grain of truth, you finally, truly take charge of a situation. Now that you are dealing with the truth, you can search for a solution that treats the cause and not the symptom.

Coach yourself with the following questions. You can ponder them out loud, journal through your answers, or talk them over with someone you trust. The goal is to peel back more layers or truth, be bold and courageous in deciding what to do to move forward with integrity.

- What issues are being caused by the grain of truth I am now acknowledging?

- In what way(s) are these issues holding me back?

- In what way(s) are these issues impacting other people?

- Is there anyone with whom I need to make amends now that I am acknowledging a grain of truth I may have previously denied, ignored, or blamed others for?

- Who can best help me resolve the problem created by the grain of truth I am now acknowledging?

- What opportunity does this challenge offer me for growth?

- What will improve if I address this issue?

- How do I want to be better as a result of pushing through this challenge?

- What are my options for rectifying this problem?

- What option(s) will I take and when?

- How will I stay accountable?

Give yourself permission to be imperfect.

Declaration

In the most basic form of the word, a declaration is an explicit statement or announcement. It indicates that the words spoken are official—a decision has been made and the full intention is now laid out. Making a personal declaration can be a powerful way to lay out your intentions and commit to a plan of action. After you admit the grain of truth, speak it, and then decide to move forward, declare your intention. Say it out loud and even write it down:

Speaking the grain of truth is a hallmark of resilience. And resilience is a hallmark of the most successful people. When you say aloud the truth you most want to ignore, you take its power away. You, in essence, say, "I see you, and I will deal with you."

You have a power at work within you when you are willing to ignite it that is greater than any circumstance or situation. But that power can only work in the light. Shine the light on the stuff you don't want to see so you can clear the way to create exactly what you really want to see.

Years ago, I was speaking to several hundred businesswomen at a luncheon in Raleigh, North Carolina, when one of my greatest professional fears unfolded as I stood onstage. To be clear, I have never been afraid of public speaking. I'm a talker. My mom has often joked that I talked so much as a kid that she would play a game with me to see how long I could go *without* talking. Two minutes was my record. But the one thing I sometimes feared was that I might forget a talking point.

I remember the scene vividly—the coral and cream tweed suit I was wearing, the month and year, the energy of the women in that room. My talk was going great. The audience was engaged. They laughed. They took notes. Everything you want to happen when you are the keynote was happening that day.

Maybe I became overly confident. Maybe I got distracted. I'm not sure of the culprit, but in midsentence in the midst of telling a story that would make a really profound point, "Poof!" My thought vanished into thin air.

I looked at the faces of the women seated at a center table directly in front of the stage. Their faces were filled with anticipation. They were listening. Some were nodding and smiling. They were ready for my next point…but I didn't have one. I threw in a couple of filler sentences thinking that if I just kept talking, I'd recapture my thought and no one would notice. But nope. Nothing.

This had never happened before, and amazingly, in hundreds of speeches since then, it has never happened again. So I didn't have a game plan for this. I had to think quickly. I was on a stage alone standing in front of 400 women whose sole job in that moment was to listen to me. There was no time to confer with a girlfriend or run back to my seat and find my notes. I pondered the thought of abandoning the story altogether and jumping to my next point. It would be choppy, but hey, by the end of the speech, they would probably forget.

But something in me said, "Just tell them the truth." So, with a smile and a laugh, I blurted out, "This is going to sound crazy, but I just totally lost my train of thought. What was I saying?"

For about three seconds, there was a pause as they processed that I was, in fact, not joking. Then, to my amazement and utter delight, at least 30 women around the room started laughing and yelling the answer to me from the audience! No judgment. Only help. They were rooting for me. And several said afterward, "I loved that you just admitted that you didn't remember what you were saying. It was so real."

Resilience requires authenticity. In the moments when we most believe we need to "have it together" and do things perfectly, it is our willingness to admit that perhaps we don't have the answer that becomes our saving grace. Giving ourselves permission to be imperfect opens the door to connect authentically with others. It lets them in, helps them see a little of themselves, and shows them how they can help us. You don't have to go it alone.

You don't have to be perfect to be successful. You just have to keep bouncing back. And it's easier to do when you admit there's something to bounce back from.

Your Script for Success

- Acknowledge the grain of truth that you wish wasn't true. When you are willing to admit the truth, you can deal with it.
- Sometimes being positive keeps you from talking about things that are negative, and that can be detrimental to your success.
- Use criticism—both constructive and destructive—to improve and grow.

Every Woman Should Know

- Speaking positively is important, but not at the expense of ignoring a negative truth. Speak truthfully about your challenges, and then speak positively about your ability to overcome them.
- The longer you ignore the truth, the more inauthentic you become.
- The biggest opportunity for growth comes when you must find courage in the face of fear.

Coach Yourself

- Think back to a recent criticism you've received but rejected. What is the grain of truth in the criticism? If you acknowledge that truth right now, what would you do differently moving forward?

- In what way(s) do you speak positively about something in your life while ignoring a negative that needs to be addressed? What would improve if you confronted the negative?

- What would you be free to do if you spoke the truth in an important relationship, career challenge, or financial move?

Speak Differently

Speak the truth about your situation, even when the truth scares or disappoints you. Being accurate is more powerful than being positive.

Show Up

*The key to changing minds and hearts
lies in this increasingly elusive habit.*

*I've learned that people will forget what you
said, people will forget what you did, but people
will never forget how you made them feel.*
MAYA ANGELOU

Key Lessons

- Your undivided attention makes communication easier.

- Warmth, trust, power, and passion cannot happen without presence.

- Your spirit cannot fake passion. Your voice and body will alert the world.

had been sitting in the doctor's office alone, twiddling my thumbs and hoping for some encouraging news when she finally walked in. She was attractive and appeared to be very knowledgeable. Unlike the doctor I'd been going to for several years who was probably three decades my senior (and very personable), this doctor looked to be just a couple of years older than me. My previous appointment had been canceled after I arrived at the doctor's office because she had apparently been caught in traffic and not made it in. This time she was in the office but running behind. I can be a pretty flexible person, but this wasn't the way I had hoped to start with my new doctor.

She looked at some test results that came back regarding my fertility. For my age, the results were quite positive. That made me feel hopeful, and I responded to the news, in part, wanting to connect. "I haven't lost hope," I said quietly. "I really believe in my heart I am going to have a baby." The coldness in her face mirrored the callousness in her demeanor. She didn't acknowledge my words and quickly pivoted the conversation to suggest I get an egg donor.

It is hard to describe the range of emotions in such a deeply personal and complicated matter, but I can say this. Her words caused me to momentarily lapse into self-doubt. In a matter of seconds while sitting in the chair next to the doctor's desk, I thought: "Maybe I am silly for trying to get pregnant at 41. Even though my mother had my brother at this age, maybe my hope is nothing but foolishness." How vulnerable it felt to pursue a dream for which the window of opportunity might be closed. I knew the odds were slim, but I had still been willing to try. Reaching out to the doctor was an important step in trying.

I know doctors often have to share difficult news with patients, and to do that without becoming emotionally drained can be hard day after day. I learned that lesson many years ago when the surgeon who had just finish my mother's emergency brain surgery casually tossed a tissue in the trash can while explaining that my mother "might be brain damaged or might not make it. We'll know in 72 hours." His delivery was casual, which made it hard to process the shocking seriousness of what he'd just said. But even so, I wouldn't have called his delivery cold. Even though I felt blindsided, for that surgeon, it was everyday business.

But this doctor's demeanor felt different. As I asked questions, she answered them with a tone that suggested I should have already known the answers. There was no trace of compassion. And so I was left feeling like just another patient to cycle through the office—a number in a long line of numbers.

Needless to say, after a few visits, I found a new doctor. And when women close to me have asked for a referral, have I suggested this doctor? Of course not. Not because she was not competent, but because I didn't like how it felt to be her patient.

It is an illustration of the power of a truth we can all learn from: It isn't what you say or what you know that endears people to you but how they feel as a result of interacting with you.

To convey the kind of warmth that influences people to trust you or send business or other opportunities your way, you must be "present" in your interactions with them. Connection happens in present moments. It happens when you acknowledge a hardship with empathy or a win with enthusiasm. It happens when you focus on another's words and tone and body language and hear what is unspoken.

To be compassionate, be present. Be with the person you are talking to—not just physically but mindfully.

The words we speak and the body language we speak must do more than convey logical information. They must convey compassion. Simply put, compassion says, "I care." It doesn't have to be sappy or overstated. It means you'll have to be present enough to pay attention not just to what you want but to what the other parties want and need as well. You'll have to take care how your words impact others.

I can only speculate as to the dynamics that led to that experience in the doctor's office that day, but I can share what I sensed during the visits I had there:

- Her schedule was treated as more important than her patients' schedules.

- She seemed unhappy. Whether with her job or something more personal, I don't know, but there was an underlying current of dissatisfaction.

- It seemed my appointment was just one more thing on a long, demanding, unenjoyable to-do list. She didn't have presence of mind because her mind was on the rest of her demands.

Many of us have had the experience of feeling this way or observed others struggling with such attitudes and emotions. Whatever the issues, the perception from the receiving end of the conversation is a lack of compassion.

Every single day we can see examples of people who are considered successful yet care only about themselves and their objectives. They don't care about others. They may even demean them or dismiss other people as less important for not having achieved the same level of "success."

Remember, true success is a harmony of purpose, resilience, and joy. It is not defined by an amount of money in your possession, a job title, or popularity. If you aren't living the life you were created to live, using your uniqueness to positively impact the world or bounce back from setbacks, and there is no joy in how you go about living, then you are not successful. It is impossible to treat people poorly and truly have joy. It is impossible to be self-centered and joyful. Our joy is inextricably connected to our ability to love and be loved, even in the smallest acts of kindness and respect in how we communicate to others.

To be compassionate, be present. Be with the person you are talking to—not just physically, but mindfully.

Opportunities to Show Up Show Up Constantly

It's Saturday afternoon, and almost as soon as I finished that last sentence, my youngest, bonus daughter, Addie, knocked on the door. "Where's Daddy?" she asked. "I want to show him the house we made for the turtle."

I had no clue what she was talking about. We don't have a turtle. Or at least, we didn't this morning. She walked over to the window in front of me and leaned on the ledge. The serious look on her face indicated she'd been working. I mean "working" in the eight-year-old sense of the word.

"What turtle?" I asked, feeling a little pressed for time as I have a specific window of time in which to write today.

"Oh, there was a turtle at the bottom of the driveway when we got back from the park," she explained. "Sophie and I are in the backyard making him a home."

"Okay, I'll tell Daddy to come down as soon as he gets off the phone," I started. But as I looked at Addie, with her pink glasses and shorts, hair blowing just slightly from the breeze coming in through the open window, I remembered what I was writing about. Being present. Being interested. And I shifted.

"I'd love to see the turtle house. Would you like to show it to me?" I said. The corners of her mouth turned up as she grinned and pushed herself up from the window ledge. "Yeah!"

I walked downstairs and joined her older sister, Sophie, at the bottom of the steps leading into the backyard. They'd built a small fort for the two-inch turtle they'd already named Tuck after the turtle in the *Wonder Pets!* series. He was swimming in a small pool of water and rocks inside one of my Tupperware containers on the edge of the fort with dirt packed around it so he could crawl in and out. I suggested the little guy might like to get out of the pool for a while, and we watched him crawl around. I told them about the time my dad and I found a turtle trying to cross the street in front of our house and kept it for the weekend. It was much bigger, I reminisced, but not nearly as cute. After a few minutes, I headed back upstairs.

It was such a simple moment. But a few years from now, we won't have such moments as they move on to more mature interests. When I write from home, I can't expect not to have interruptions or I'll be repeatedly disappointed. But when I get those interruptions, I can be intentional about how I make my family feel. Do they feel like a bother, or do they feel like I have time for them?

This isn't to say we shouldn't have boundaries or that people should be able to have our time whenever they want. But if I can't make my daughter know I'm interested in what she has to say when she talks to me about a new childhood masterpiece because I am too busy working, then I am sending a message that is counter to my definition of success for our relationship.

Deadlines and stress and overwhelm can suck the compassion right out of our communication habits. We can become irritable with people because we are frustrated at how much is on our plates. Or we can be present one moment at a time. We can do what we can. We can prioritize relationships over the screen in front of us. We can be present.

If you want to be effective in your communication,
be the person who is present.

How Do People Feel in Your Presence?

When you aren't fully present, even if you try your best to pretend you are, it shows. There is really no way to hide it. When your mind is elsewhere and you are mulling over your to-do list while feigning attentiveness to the person who is speaking to you, your facial expressions will be slightly delayed. Even though you are looking directly into the eyes of the other person, your eyes might even glaze over.

Our brains read facial expressions so quickly that we ourselves don't always understand the reason we don't think someone is fully present or worthy of our trust. We can perceive a problem without conscious awareness of the information our brain has processed that alerted us something was off. Letting your mind wander or multitasking won't encourage anyone to feel listened to, supported, or valued in your presence. It speaks the message, "I have more important things to do or think about in this moment."

With the amount of stimuli most of us endure in any given moment, being present in your conversations with others can be really challenging. You are apt to be interrupted by a text message or email chime or phone call, or lured to distraction by social media, online surfing, or television. Maintaining awareness in the moment of a conversation is more challenging than it has ever been. Add to that this interesting tidbit: Your brain actively seeks out inconsistencies in your environment. Anything that doesn't look like it belongs, anything that sounds different or is new in any way, gets your attention quickly. Why? Because before the conveniences and protections of modern society, not noticing such things might result in your being caught by surprise by a deadly animal or walking into a dangerous situation.

So today we are overwhelmed by distractions and find ourselves constantly attempting to pay a little bit of attention to multiple things. What does that mean for how people feel in your presence? It means that if you can learn to give your full attention to the moment and person in front of you and then move on to the next when you are finished, people will experience a feeling with you that they rarely experience: feeling heard. Few people today feel listened to and, hence, important enough to command anyone's full attention. If you want to be effective in your communication, be the person who is present.

Success Emerges from Passion— Passion Emerges from Presence

In my travels to speaking engagements, I sometimes encounter intriguing people. In 2015, while speaking at a convention in Denver, I met Julie Terrell, whose story has intrigued me for some time. Hers is a testimony of the power of simple passion—the kind of authenticity that makes people want to join in the vision. When that happens, there is no limit to the possibilities for real success.

It was July 2013, and Julie Terrell, wife and mother of four, was worrying aloud over lunch with a friend and mentor. She and her husband, Nathan, had been Christian missionaries in a small town in the mountains of Mexico since their first child was a baby. And they'd come home to Colorado for a couple of months to earn extra money, something they sometimes did to play financial catch-up. But this time, after years of subsisting on $800 to $1200 a month for a family of six, she had suddenly awakened to a persistent question.

"As my oldest was school age, I started thinking about the things they'd need as they got older," Julie explained. "How would we pay for braces if they needed them? How would we send them to college?" These were the questions she shared aloud with her friend that summer day over lunch.

Her friend gave her some deeply spiritual advice. "Go to your dad," Julie recalls her friend saying casually. Julie quickly batted down the idea. She wasn't asking her parents to give them money.

"I don't mean your earthly father," her friend clarified. "I mean your heavenly Father. Have you prayed and asked Him for what you need?"

Julie had not. She thought it was a bit selfish to pray for money when so many of the families they served every day had so much less. But she accepted the challenge and tried. Every day for about two weeks she spoke to God about her worries. With guilt on her conscience about asking for more than she already felt blessed with, she started small. Like, really small.

"I spent the first couple of days praying for other people's needs. And then I finally decided to ask for something for my family. It sounds crazy, but I prayed for enough money to buy cheddar cheese," she said. A block of cheddar cheese was very expensive in the area where they lived—about $9. A few days later, she got really bold and asked for enough money to get rid of a couple thousand dollars of debt they had accumulated. Soon, she worked her way to asking God to open a door of opportunity to make more money.

For many women, those requests seem quite reasonable. But for Julie, there were many doubts and obstacles to the possibility she could contribute to her family's financial well-being. She was raised in an ultraconservative faith community where she was taught that her mission in life was to get married and have babies. She wasn't allowed to go to college. She and her husband's families had brought them together and approved their marriage. Life was pretty much laid out for her with very few thoughts of a personal mission or vision. Praying these prayers was an act of faith, and it required the presence of mind to press through insecurities, guilt, and old beliefs.

After about two weeks of praying, Julie says she felt a sense of peace come over her. It was as though God said, "I've got this. Don't worry."

A week or so later, her baby sister asked her to help with a goal. She had joined a direct sales company called Jamberry that sells nail wraps—vinyl adhesive nails that can be applied with heat to create a manicure that lasts two to three weeks. Her sister wanted to make a "fast start" goal, selling a certain amount of product and recruiting a few interested friends to join her in selling the product.

Julie didn't pay much attention to the product. In fact, she didn't try it for almost a month. Then she started posting about it on Facebook and sold some of the product online after she returned to Mexico. She never left her house. Within 30 days, she'd earned more than $400.

"I couldn't believe it," Julie remembers. "I had increased our household income by almost 50 percent in one month. So I started thinking, 'Who else could I tell? I mean I knew a lot of stay-at-home moms whose families needed to earn more money. I just messaged them and said, 'Hey, you should check this out. I made $400 in one month and I was able to do it from home.'" Before she knew it, friends were signing up.

"I didn't even think of it as recruiting. I was just excited. It was blessing my family, and I thought they should know about it in case they wanted to try it too."

That was fall. And by Christmas, her monthly check was more than $1000. She became more intentional about identifying more women to talk to. "I became a team manager by December," she explains. Her checks doubled every month after that. Today Julie has a downline of approximately 22,000 sales consultants. Of more than 100,000 consultants in the company, only 33 have reached the highest rank. Julie is one of them, and that transpired in less than two years. To say her prayers were answered is an understatement.

"Our tax adviser said, 'I just want to warn you, you will be audited. In a year and a half, your household income surged from $20,000 to over $1,000,000.'"

They can buy a whole lot more than cheddar cheese now. And they started wondering, "There's got to be more that God wants us to do with this money than just invest it for ourselves." In 2016, their transition from the mission field of Mexico to the mission field of the United States began. The vision has grown from "enough money to buy cheddar cheese" to "enough to pay off debt" to "Who can we bless?"

"Our goal is a ranch for girls who have been rescued or escaped from the sex trafficking trade," she explains. They are moving to North Texas to do just that—create a nonprofit that will provide education and resources to help victims transition to healthy, thriving lives. It is a dream bigger than their bank account.

She started early in the company's history when few had heard of the product. She has said to me on several occasions, "It wasn't me. I didn't really do anything." And I know where she is coming from. As a humble woman of faith, she would never lose sight that this was the answer at the end of those two weeks of prayer that began with a request for God to give them enough wiggle room in their budget to buy cheddar cheese. But it was also due to some specific ways in which she spoke differently—she showed up fully. Here's how:

- She spoke to a mentor about her concerns. She took the advice humbly.

- She voiced her desires in faith. She didn't know how it would happen, but her mindset shifted when she had the audacity to open her mouth and pray for more.

- She didn't murmur and complain, even while living below the poverty line.

- She expressed gratitude for her blessings when she had very little.

- She genuinely loved the product. She engaged with it. She showed up fully and had fun with it. The shape and length of her nails are a pretty showcase for the Jamberry product, and she shared lots of photos and videos of her beautiful nails. Her appearance spoke volumes.

- She spoke enthusiastically and authentically about how she was being blessed because she wanted to see others blessed too.

- Her online presence is energetic and positive, yet authentic. She smiles. She encourages.

- "I can't believe I get paid to help women" was one of Julie's comments to me. She communicates nonstop. But in every communication, there is an attitude of service, concern, and compassion. Such presence has yielded her an enthusiastic team of thousands of women.

How to Build More Presence in Your Relationships

Here are a few ways to build a sense of presence when you speak to and listen to others. Try these in your next interaction.

- Laser focus on the person with whom you are in conversation.

- Tune out distractions. Behave as though they are not there.

- Stop thinking about what you are going to say next and listen.

It isn't just external stimuli that can be distracting. It is also the internal dialogue about the point you want to make next that can divert your attention. It can take you out of the present moment. Your mind wanders to wanting to sound clever or right or funny or however you imagine you need to sound. If you truly listen though, your full presence will guide you to the next right words to speak in the conversation.

If you are uptight about the things you feel you need to be doing but aren't because you are engaged in conversation, it will show. Either make the decision to be fully present or move the conversation to another time.

Have you ever felt stressed by a conversation because you were pressed for time? You rushed the conversation or felt irritated while having the conversation. These may be normal reactions to an overloaded schedule, but they will sabotage your relationships and your success. No one wants to feel they are a bother or a hindrance, keeping you from other things. And if they feel that way often enough, it isn't a matter of whether there will be consequences. It is a matter of when.

When this happens, it is an opportunity to pause and reflect. Do you need to delegate or delay some to-dos that are on your list? Do you need to be honest about your mental state and tell someone how important they are and how you want to give them more of your attention but need to come up with a better time? Or do you need to exercise some self-control and give the person in front of you your full attention right now? Being present doesn't necessarily mean spending excessive amounts of time with each person with whom you interact. Instead, it is about being present in the interactions, even short ones. It is being intentional: You have chosen to interact with this person, and they will feel valued in your presence. They will remember what it feels like to interact with you, even if they cannot put their finger on the reason why.

When you feel your stress rising and the pressure of talking to one more person overwhelming you, pause, take a deep breath, and reflect. Rein in your thoughts of "not enough time" and make a decision to value the person and time that is before you in this moment. Utter a prayer to melt the anxiety, and watch how quickly you are able to shift your focus:

> *In this moment, what I ask for is focus. Help me relax and focus on the person in front of me right now. Help me trust that if I engage fully in each interaction, not only will it benefit the other person, ultimately my future will be better for it. Help me remember that my interactions are for a purpose greater than my to-do list. People may not remember everything I say, but they will certainly remember how they feel in my presence. Help me give them a glimpse of You.*

Pressed for Time

As someone who went from single with no children to married with three children in under two years, I've come to appreciate the preciousness of time on a new level. Add to that a move from the city to the outskirts of the suburbs, and the idea of getting together for lunch or dinner takes on new meaning. I can't do it, at least not if my family priorities are to stay intact. So when I get together with someone, it is never haphazard. It is purposeful. I find myself treasuring the time together. Most of my time is invested in my family and my business, so when I carve out time for someone outside of those two priorities, I savor the moment. Conversations feel richer to me. I am more likely to express appreciation or get to the heart of a matter that's pressing. I'm more alive in conversation because I am more aware of the gift of that moment.

Rather than feeling pressed for time, you can feel grateful for moments to connect—even small ones. Life may sometimes feel overwhelming, but giving thanks for the fullness of it and what that fullness represents is a powerful way to remain present. Yes, evenings may feel packed tight with meals and homework and extracurricular activities, but this is a unique season you'll look back on years later. How do you want to remember it? What will you wish you could have told your younger self? Work projects may cause stress, but what is the message being offered to you in the midst of it all? There is a gift in the stress. Unwrap it. It might be a message that you are being stretched for greater opportunities in the future. It may be the nudge toward a new path, one that creates less stress in your life. Or maybe it is the message that it's time to stop sweating the small stuff.

When you learn to manage the thoughts that cause you to feel pressed and stressed, you completely change how you feel in the moment. And that change transforms how you interact with others. When stressed, the natural human response is self-protection. And when your thoughts are absorbed with yourself, they cannot be focused on compassion toward others. You can't give what you don't have.

But I would like to suggest something more. We don't need to be intentional only about how our words—and the way we say them—make others feel. We should be intentional about the compassion we show for ourselves too.

The Power of Self-Compassion

Researchers are now exploring self-compassion. For high achievers, and especially overachievers (and if you are reading a book about successful women, there is a strong possibility one of these terms describes you), self-compassion is rarer than simple compassion. It is quite common that a woman who is very compassionate toward others and with whom others feel valued, loved, and heard, can have an unusually difficult time being compassionate toward herself. How you speak to yourself matters. It can either ease your stress or exacerbate it. It can cause you to learn from your mistakes or beat yourself up indefinitely for them.

The most successful women—those who not only live with purpose and are resilient but also have a lot of joy in their lives—are also compassionate toward themselves in moments of inadequacy. In the face of a mistake or failure, they treat themselves much as you would treat your best friend. The opposite is true for other women, whose treatment of themselves does not resemble the way they might nurture, support, or encourage someone they care about.

Researcher and educational psychologist Kristin Neff, Ph.D., of the University of Texas at Austin, says self-compassion is composed of three elements—self-kindness, common humanity, and mindfulness.

"Be gentle with yourself," my friend said sweetly. "You're so hard on yourself." As the sound of her words fell softly on my ears, they resonated deeply. It was what I needed to hear. It sounded like something I should be saying to her, not vice versa. I mean, after all, I'm the life coach, the author who writes about happiness, and resilience, and authenticity. But it is often easier to identify a need in someone else than it is to recognize the need in yourself. I took a deep breath and closed my eyes. "Thank you," I said. "I needed that."

Sometimes, what you need most is a gentle voice giving you permission to be human. Permission to fall short without the threat of being beaten up for it. Sometimes that voice comes from a friend. More often than not, that voice must come from you. Your voice has the power to remind you that success is a harmony of purpose, resilience, and joy. Every experience serves a purpose, molding you more beautifully into a woman of wisdom. Every time you fall short, you are offered the opportunity to be resilient and get back up again. It is the imperfect perfection of resilience to look back and see that the only way to arrive at the current destination was to take the detour that led you along your divinely orchestrated path. And every time you show up fully—with the warmth of authenticity, the truth of transparency, and the enthusiasm that can only come from your passion—you move the world with your most powerful voice.

Understand the Power of "Liking"

*How three simple habits can build your
influence and multiply your success*

Key Lessons

- Showing people you care leads to greater influence over their lives.

- Focus on what you have in common with others to grow your relationship with them.

- Your degree of optimism can shape your future success.

W hat is influence? And how much of it do you have—at work, at home, or when faced with a situation you want to work in your favor?

Your influence is your capacity to have an effect on someone's character, development, or behavior.[1] You've probably noticed some women around you who seem to wield more influence than others. People are won to their point of view more easily, seem to follow their lead even if they are not in positions of leadership, and clamber to get what they have to offer.

One could argue that influence has been women's secret leadership weapon over the course of history. Locked out of opportunities and official leadership titles, women of past generations had to creatively find ways to influence decisions and changes even if they did not have the authority to make those decisions. Even today, with so many more women in official positions of leadership than ever before, I have observed that many women who do not identify themselves as "leaders" are quick to acknowledge their own ability to influence others. If you influence others, you are a leader.

So just what do the most influential women do differently than other women? Do they really just speak differently? And if so, how?

Influence is largely about what causes people to say yes to your viewpoint, your request, or your idea. Let's talk about a few key habits that can transform your ability to "get to yes"—whether you want to be hired for a job, generate interest in a project, or get a team on board with your idea. These habits are showing concern for those around you, making people like you, and being generous with your approval, appreciation, and acknowledgments.

Showing Concern for Those Around You

It almost sounds too simple, but it's a simple fact that caring leads to influence. Theodore Roosevelt famously said, "Nobody cares how much you know until they know how much you care."

The people who show concern for you, who go out of their way for you and display an interest in what matters to you, are the people who are most likely to influence you. I once had a boss who handwrote personalized birthday cards to every employee in the company. It seems like a small gesture, and it is, but the positive emotions it created in each person strengthened the relationship between the leader and those who followed her.

Now, imagine for a moment that your boss remembers all of your children's names and ages, routinely stops by your desk and asks about them, and then listens as you talk about them. Imagine that same boss tells you about a skill you need to develop and opens up an opportunity for you to be trained on that particular skill. Imagine there is a death in the family, and the boss has your company cater meals for your family after the funeral as a gesture of support.

All of these are real scenarios, and guess what? All the bosses who engaged in these acts of care and concern have fiercely loyal employees. They have employees who absolutely do not mind going the extra mile for their boss. They enjoy going to work and voluntarily suggest creative ideas that save the company money and increase sales. These bosses influence the behavior of their team not by telling them what to do differently, but by caring.

People are loyal when they feel they matter. Want more proof? The Values in Action Character Strengths Survey is a tool that helps you discover and understand your signature strengths.[2] Your strengths might include teamwork, creativity, gratitude, or perseverance. It seems counterintuitive, but one of the most common signature strengths of effective leaders isn't leadership, but another strength—one hardly anyone would guess: "The capacity to love and be loved."

What does love have to do with leadership? A whole lot, really. Who wouldn't want to follow a leader they felt personally cared about them? If you believe your leader cares about you, you can trust their leadership decisions. You'll go out of your way to support their ideas and bring their vision to life. Love is such a refreshing way to feel about a leader that you may even feel inspired. And the ability to inspire is another distinct trait of effective leaders. So if you want to influence a particular group or person, stop and ask yourself, *Have I connected with them by showing my care and concern for the things that matter most to them?*

Love speaks powerfully. Love influences.

There is probably no better demonstration of this concept than the church. Christians often believe that witnessing to nonbelievers by *telling* them about their faith is the way to win people to Christ. But talk is just talk. Your words may be heartfelt, gripping, and inspirational, but sharing your faith through your actions is more powerful by far.

The first Christians were eleven disciples and a handful of believers. But Jesus's followers multiplied, and today there are estimated to be more than 2 billion believers in the world. How did such a small number of people influence a faith to multiply so dramatically and endure more than 2000 years?

Historians point to one period in particular. Around 250 AD, the Plague of Cyprian, a pandemic now believed to be smallpox, swept through the Roman Empire. At the height of the outbreak, it is estimated that 5000 people per day were dying of the plague in Rome. It created a shortage of workers in agriculture and the military, causing both a famine in the land and a dearth in security. People left their own

family members on the street to die in efforts to keep from dying themselves or losing other family members to the illness. It raged on for an
unbelievable number of years—about two decades. And during that
time, Christianity began to *grow*.

Why? Because third-century Christians actually practiced what the
Bible preaches with regard to love. They were the only people who
stayed and cared for the sick when others abandoned them. And they
did so not because they had special access to medicines to prevent them
from contracting the disease. They did so because they wanted to display the kind of love their Savior had shown for them.

Love speaks powerfully. Love influences.

Early Christians, through their courageous love in the face of death,
influenced those who followed pagan gods to become curious about
Jesus. It didn't happen because they talked about their God. It happened because they allowed their God to show up in how they chose
to love others. And that influence multiplied the number of Christians.

So how about you? In what ways could your love and care for others increase your influence in the situations that matter most in this
season of your life? Brainstorm some ideas below.

- At work

- With your children

- With your spouse or significant other

- In your neighborhood

- At church

Your true power comes from seeking common ground.

Making People Like You

Ever think about the seeming absurdity of politicians kissing babies? Or rolling up their sleeves and going to a local pub or bowling alley for a photo op? Why do they take pictures with their whole families? I mean, the job they're applying for will not require the input of the spouse or children, nor any babysitting or bowling tournaments. So why bother?

The reason is that people are more likely to vote for someone they like, and we make decisions about liking people based on their appearance, what we have in common with them, and whether they affirm our own decisions and positions.

The whole idea of "liking" as an important foundation for building influence may sound superficial, but it's how we are wired as humans. And by understanding the process of how people come to a place of "liking," you dramatically increase your chances to succeed, to have doors open more easily, and to have greater influence in the world around you.

I am not suggesting that you make it your objective to be liked to the detriment of your character, beliefs, or authenticity. Not everyone will like you. It's okay. Being liked should not be your life's work. The best rule of thumb is to be your best self. Seek in any given moment to be kind, authentic, and helpful.

Your best self won't look the same every day. Some days you have more energy, more inspiration. Other days you may not feel well or may be discouraged or stressed. You're human. But even on your worst days, there is still a best version of you in that state. It's not as great as your best self on your best days. But it's a whole lot better than your worst self on your worst days!

So do your best. And remember this: Your ability to influence people is directly correlated with whether or not they like you. And research shows that simple shifts and behaviors create a sense of "liking." This is not to suggest that you should rearrange your life to make people like you, but you should be aware of the impact of your actions and behaviors on people. Where you are able to make shifts that feel authentic for you, do it.

When it comes to your ability to influence other people's behavior and decisions, whether or not a person likes you can be a major determining factor. But what makes someone like you? Research shows that a major component of "liking" is having commonalities. We like people who are like us in some way. This can be as simple as a cue taken from the fact that you are wearing a similar outfit or you grew up in the same region of the country or voted for the same presidential candidate. Even small things can make a difference in how comfortable someone feels around you and is ultimately approved of by you.

Finding common ground is a key to influencing others. Going out of your way to point out how you are different from others is a sure way to have less influence on them. Develop a habit of noticing common experiences, interests, or background with people. In a world where we are often encouraged to divide ourselves by differences, stake out territories, and fight over those differences, you will discover that your true power comes from finding common ground.

Your ability to influence people is directly correlated
with whether or not they like you.

I run a program dedicated to training personal and executive coaches.[3] One of our first training exercises is called a Positive Introduction, in which students who will practice coaching each other in class introduce each other by sharing a pivotal challenge in their lives. They describe the challenge—sometimes a life-altering moment such as overcoming a divorce, bouncing back from a loss of some sort, or handling a difficult career move—and explain how the challenge somehow made them a better person. They do this in a matter of minutes in a small cohort of three or four people in the first hour of a three-day training.

What happens in the room is phenomenal. At every training we've conducted since launching the Coach Training Intensive in 2010, students say one thing in particular: "We learned that we have so much in common. It is no accident I happened to sit next to the people I sat next to. Our stories show how similar we are in spirit." It is an important exercise *before* the students begin coaching because they need to see each other at their core before they can trust each other in the context of a coaching session. Alikeness builds a sense of trust. "You understand me. You've been through something I can relate to, and you emerged stronger for it."

Here's something I learned growing up in a military family and living overseas as a child. Being in environments where people did not look like me or even speak the same language as me forced me out of the comfort zone of obvious similarities. When you walk out of your house knowing that most of the people on your street speak a different language, you can either get hung up on that fact or you can open your eyes and begin to notice the larger human commonalities you share. Perhaps your nationality and language and culture and skin color are not the same, but your love of family and strawberries and Christmas traditions are undeniably alike. It was a training ground for spotting commonalities. And there began my intrigue with cultures and language and people. Overfocusing on differences narrows your influence. But when you focus on commonalities, your influence grows.

Let me share an example. I speak often and all over the country—and sometimes outside of the country. I am frequently asked a question, especially by pastors and people of faith. "I think it is very interesting that you speak to major corporations and government agencies, and even on national television shows, but you also speak in churches," they point out. "How do you do that?"

Now, this isn't something I mapped out. In fact, I don't see the various venues as all that different. Everywhere I speak, I am speaking to *people*. People need to know how to be resilient. They want more success—purpose, resilience, and joy. They want to be happy, and I talk a lot about what it takes to boost your happiness. These subjects are equally relevant if I'm making an appearance on a network morning show or speaking to executives at a major national bank or sharing with women at a church conference. In fact, some of the women at the church conference or sitting at home watching the network morning show also work at the bank!

I don't limit my influence by approaching my message as though it is meant for only one audience. My mission is inspiring women to live more fulfilling lives—not inspiring just corporate women, or women at church, or women of one race. My calling integrates all elements of who I am as a woman—a businesswoman, a woman of faith, a woman of color, and now, a happy wife and mom. I write and speak best when I communicate fluidly from all of those perspectives. If I focus on the differences, I narrow my influence.

The practice of seeing the commonalities between you and others may require a bit of optimistic thinking. This idea falls in line with the research that optimism is a predictor of success. If optimism helps us see the good—and as a result, see commonalities—then it is reasonable to suggest that choosing an optimistic stance toward finding common ground will increase your likability, thereby increasing your influence. By the same token, seeing yourself as more separate from others than connected—and seeing differences as negatives—has the potential to decrease your likability as people mirror what you reflect back to them.

It isn't that differences are bad. We have differences. This is what makes us interesting and diverse. It is when you inherently view "different" as a negative that you distance yourself from others and decrease your influence.

How is this idea of focusing on commonalities rather than

differences relevant in your life? How does it show up in your work? How about your friendships? Is it time to broaden your perspective? Jot down any inklings that may be coming to you:

When others look for reasons to "like" you by looking for commonalities, the similarities do not have to be significant. Think back to a time when you saw someone wearing a sweater or shoes or pair of earrings that were just like something you owned. There was an automatic positive response. Little points of connection create a doorway to liking.

When you stop and think about it, what does it signal when someone is dressed like you? At its core, commonalities are a small form of validation.[4] So when you have something in common, in a way, it affirms your own choices and experiences. It creates the feeling that you are not alone, that another person has shared your experience.

Commonalities are just one path to liking, though. Another path to liking that builds the likelihood of more influence is a more direct form of validation—appreciation and approval.

> *When you inherently view "different" as a negative, you distance yourself from others and decrease your influence.*

Being Generous with Your Approval, Appreciation, and Acknowledgments

A good compliment is not only kind. It is wise. Those who freely give compliments create a dynamic that makes them more likable. And research confirms that even when people say that compliments don't matter to them, those compliments actually increase the likelihood they will say yes to future requests.[5] Giving approval in the form of compliments, affirmation, and acknowledgment builds the bonds that strengthen your influence.

Research has shown time and again that it is more powerful to build on one's strengths than to try to fix one's weaknesses.[6] In fact, in the workplace, it is critical for managers to acknowledge what employees do well and not just harp on what needs to be improved. We all like to hear good things about ourselves, and it appears that affirming a person's good attributes is the right way to get them to make needed changes. But in the most basic way, using your words to compliment others increases their liking of you and makes them more open to hearing and being influenced by what you have to say.

In fact, if you want to influence the likelihood of a person repeating a behavior or saying yes to a request, state your compliment in a way that gives them a reputation to live up to. For example, "So-and-so told me you did a fantastic job with that project, and I would love it if you would consider helping on this new project," or, "The way you decorated your house is stunning. I am hoping you'll be willing to give me some advice and insights on my own home." It is a natural inclination that we want to live up to the praise we've been given, so our actions are often driven to maintain consistency between past decisions and "wins" and future ones. Complimenting positive behavior, therefore, not only increases your likability with the person being complimented, but also influences the likelihood that behavior will be repeated.

Positive emotion—like the emotional boost that comes from hearing positive things said about ourselves—is known to broaden our scope of thinking and open our minds to making better, more creative decisions.[7] If you want to increase your influence, praise the good you see in people. Compliment them. Notice what they do well. Be sincere. Don't flatter. Make it a game to find things you can authentically affirm and compliment. Not only does it feel good to give the compliments and see how they light up others, but it simultaneously creates a stronger response from them to other ideas you share.

My client Vanessa ran a retail shop that had a minimal online presence but was not active in marketing online sales. As a result, the online store generated a small amount of revenue. She knew it could do better, but she had no time to focus on it. She also didn't have much of a budget to hire someone.

She considered her existing team of eight employees. They were all good employees, but one in particular seemed to have the potential to be groomed for the role. She decided to enlist Michael, one of her sales associates, to increase the online sales revenue. Michael was easygoing, finishing up his college degree in business, and very comfortable with technology.

When Michael came on board with the new responsibility of boosting sales online, she complimented him strongly at the weekly meeting with her small team of associates. She emphasized to the group how she was certain that with Michael's natural sales ability, his strong rapport with customers, his creativity, and his business studies degree, he'd boost their online store business in no time.

Michael's efforts started to pay off almost immediately. Every week, Vanessa would tout the sales results at the team meeting. The team would clap and congratulate Michael, and soon they started pitching ideas of their own for promotions. Many were very creative. Michael loved the affirmation. As time went on and the sales promotions increased online revenue, Vanessa's weekly announcements gave Michael something to live up to. Her acknowledgment of his success in his new role influenced him to work harder.

Favor

There is one more key habit of influence, and it is not a habit that you control. It is unmerited favor. Have you ever had good fortune come your way, but you cannot explain why it came to you or perhaps even how? That's favor. Perhaps you can relate.

The best opportunities in my career have not happened because I knew the opportunity existed and went after it. Instead, the best opportunities have shown up unannounced at a time when I was prepared to take advantage of them. For example, I received a call one afternoon to gauge my interest to replace the cohost of an Emmy-winning inspirational talk show in its tenth season. A sales manager from my publishing house knew a producer at the show and mentioned me to her in conversation. One thing led to another and before long, I found myself on the phone with the executive producer who explained the first shoot would be overseas in a location I'd dreamed of visiting for more than a decade: Israel.

Now, it can be easily argued that I worked hard to put myself in a position to be considered for such an opportunity. I spent two years doing a weekly segment on a local NBC affiliate in Dallas, I cohosted another show previously, and I studied broadcast journalism in graduate school. But the fact remains, I knew no one at this show and still they decided in short order that I was the right host. I didn't have an inside track. They had been working for years on the possibility of the shoot in Israel, but it finally all came together just before I came on board. You could call it all a coincidence. I call it something else.

It would be arrogant of me to believe that every good thing that has come into my life has been a result of my efforts, experience, or education. It isn't all a result of my contacts and my action steps. Yes, I work hard. I believe big. I do my best to maintain healthy relationships. But some doors I cannot open on my own. Some doors I don't even realize exist! And yet someone came along and hollered, "Hey, Val! Over here! There's an open door with your name on it." I call that divine favor. And I pray for it regularly.

To be clear, favor doesn't require you to be perfect—only faithful. That means when you stumble, you do your best to learn the lesson. You are willing to admit your faults and you try to do better next time. And sometimes favor comes not as a result of even your own attitude and faithfulness, but someone else's. It can be the result of your relationship with others who have been faithful. Lots of unmerited favor comes as a result of having a parent or a spouse or a friend whose favor overflows into your life, blessing you in ways you could never have influenced on your own.

Proverbs 3:3-4 tells us, "Let love and faithfulness never leave you; bind them around your neck, write them on the tablet of your heart. Then you will win favor and a good name in the sight of God and man." In other words, when you love well and live faithfully, you will win favor. Favor can give you influence when it seems you shouldn't have any. Favor can cause folks to lean your way and listen when logic says there's someone with more expertise. Favor can promote you to the position when you didn't hold the qualifications the job called for. Favor will cause people to like you, elevate you, and place you in positions of higher influence. Ask for it.

To distill the nine habits in this book for your next critical conversation, remember this:

1. **Start with the end in mind.**

   Plan your conversation. Know your goal before you start. Ask, "What is it that I want to know by the end of this conversation that I don't know now?" Then you can steer the conversation toward your goal, and you'll know when the conversation is complete.

2. **Breathe before you speak.**

   Breathing does at least three important things for your ability to speak effectively: It relaxes you, helps you become present, and strengthens your vocal essence—the sound and quality of your voice.

3. **Just say it.**

   Fear is what keeps you from speaking up. When it is time to say what needs to be said, just open your mouth and say it. Be kind, but be direct. Success requires courage. Courage empowers you to say what needs to be said.

4. **Give respect, expect respect.**

   One of the most powerful ways you can use your voice and strengthen your relationships is to set clear boundaries—an expectation of what's acceptable and what isn't. Honor others' boundaries and speak respectfully to others and of others. When you are disrespected, make the boundary clear. If needed, remove yourself from the conversation until respect can be given.

5. **Ask the powerful question, then shhhhh…**

Clarify matters by asking questions. Negotiate by asking questions. Find solutions by asking questions. Then listen to the answers and hear the essence of what is being said.

6. **Don't be afraid of silence.**

Silence is the space where information and emotions are processed. Don't fill it with nervous energy by talking aimlessly to cover it up. Be confident that out of the silence, a breakthrough can emerge.

7. **Show up fully.**

Your presence is powerful. Tune out the distractions. Give your whole heart, your whole attention, and your whole self to your conversations. It will transform your relationships. It transforms how others see you and empowers new levels of success and happiness to unfold.

NOTES

You Are Capable of Far More Than You Know

1. "Men's Honest Overconfidence May Lead to Male Domination in the G-Suite," *Columbia Business School Newsroom*, http://www8.gsb.columbia.edu/newsroom/newsn/1879/men8217s -honest-overconfidence-may-lead-to-male-domination-in-the-c8211suite.

Habit One: Sound like a Success

1. Yana Skorobogatov, "What's Up with Upspeak?" Berkeley University of California, September 21, 2015, http://www.matrix.berkeley.edu/research/whats-upspeak.

2. Robin Lakoff, "Language and Woman's Place," *Language in Society* 2, no. 1 (April 1973): 45-80.

3. 1 Chris R. Sawyer and Ralph R. Behnke, "State Anxiety Patterns for Public Speaking and the Behavior Inhibition System," *Communication Reports* 12, no. 1 (1999): 33-41, doi: 10.1080/08934219909367706.

4. Alice Robb, "Women Get Interrupted More—Even by Other Women," *New Republic,* May 14, 2014, https://newrepublic.com/article/117757/gender-language-differences-women-get-interrupted-more.

5. Cited in Rebecca Camber, "Why Women Who Want to Get Ahead Develop a Husky Voice," *Daily Mail*, June 5, 2006, http://www.dailymail.co.uk/femail/article-389130.

6. Amy Drahota, Alan Costall, and Vasudevi Reddy, "The Vocal Communication of Different Kinds of Smile," *Speech Communication* 50, no. 4 (March 2008): 278-87, doi: 10.1016/j.specom.2007.10.001.

Habit Two: What You Say Without Saying a Word

1. M. Iwase et al., "Neural Substrates of Human Facial Expression of Pleasant Emotion Induced by Comic Films: A PET Study," *Neuroimage* 17, no. 2 (October 2002): 758-68, http://www.ncbi.nlm.nih.gov/pubmed/12377151.

2. Especially notable is the work of Dr. Barbara Fredrickson of the University of North Carolina, who is renowned for her research on the effects of positive emotion on human behavior.

3. Sonja Lyubomirsky, Laura King, and Ed Diener, "The Benefits of Frequent Positive Affect: Does Happiness Lead to Success?" *Psychological Bulletin* 131, no. 6 (2005): 803-55, doi: 10.1037/0033-2909.131.6.803.

4. Amy Cuddy, *Presence* (New York: Little, Brown and Company, 2015).

5. Avi Dor et al., "A Heavy Burden: The Individual Costs of Being Overweight and Obese in the United States," The George Washington University School of Public Health and Health Services Department of Health Policy, September 21, 2010, http://publichealth.gwu.edu/departments/healthpolicy/DHP_Publications/pub_uploads/dhpPublication_35308C47-5056-9D20 3DB157B39AC53093.pdf.

6. LisaMarie Luccioni, "2010 Resolution: Dress Like a Power Player (Part III)," *Psychology Today*, February 15, 2010, https://www.psychologytoday.com/blog/the-image-professor/201002/2010-resolution-dress-power-player-part-iii.

7. Nancy L. Etcoff, Shannon Stock, Lauren E. Haley, Sarah A. Vickery, and David M. House: "Cosmetics as a Feature of the Extended Human Phenotype: Modulation of the Perception of Biologically Important Facial Signals," *PLoS ONE* 6, no. 10 (October 2011): doi:10.1371/journal.pone.0025656.

Habit Three: Learn to Flip the Script

1. "How Rick Warren's *Purpose Driven Life* Changed Former Hostage Ashley Smith," *Huffington Post*, February 25, 2013, http://www.huffingtonpost.com/2013/02/25/rick-warren-purpose-driven-life-ashley-smith_n_2741976.html.

2. Complementarity has been studied extensively by Michigan State University professor Chris Hopwood.

3. Allison Wood Brooks, "Get Excited: Reappraising Pre-Performance Anxiety as Excitement," *Journal of Experimental Psychology* 143, no. 3 (2014): 1144-58, doi: 10.1037/a0035325.

Habit Four: Build Trust Through Respect

1. Elizabeth Bernstein, "Why Good Storytellers Are Happier in Life and in Love," *The Wall Street Journal*, July 4, 2016, http://www.wsj.com/articles/why-good-storytellers-are-happier-in-life-and-in-love-1467652052.

Habit Six: Ask for What You Want

1. Katty Kay and Claire Shipman, "The Confidence Gap," *The Atlantic*, May 2014, http://www.theatlantic.com/magazine/archive/2014/05/the-confidence-gap/359815/.

Habit Seven: Know What Not to Say

1. Jon Ronson, "How One Stupid Tweet Blew Up Justine Sacco's Life," *New York Times Magazine*, February 12, 2015, http://www.nytimes.com/2015/02/15/magazine/how-one-stupid-tweet-ruined-justine-saccos-life.html.

Afterword: Understand the Power of "Liking"

1. Oxford English Dictionary.

2. You can take this survey yourself at VIAcharacter.org. These signature strengths are also discussed in greater detail in my book *Happy Women Live Better*.

3. You can learn more about this program, the Coaching and Positive Psychology Institute, at www.cappinstitute.com.

4. Jerry M. Burger et al., "What a Coincidence! The Effects of Incidental Similarity on Compliance," *Personality and Social Psychology Bulletin* 30, no. 1 (January 2004): 35-43, doi: 10.1177/0146167203258838.

5. David Drachman, Andre deCarufel, and Chester A. Insko, "The Extra Credit Effect in Interpersonal Attraction," *Journal of Experimental Social Psychology* 14, no. 5 (September 1978): 458-65, doi: 10.1016/0022-1031(78)90042-2.

6. Brian Brim and Jim Asplund, "Driving Engagement by Focusing on Strengths, *Business Journal*, November 12, 2009, http://www.gallup.com/businessjournal/124214/driving-engagement-focusing-strengths.aspx.

7. Barbara L. Fredrickson and Christine Branigan, "Positive Emotions Broaden the Scope of Attention and Thought-Action Repertoires," *Cognition and Emotion* 19, no. 3 (2005): 313-32, doi: 10.1080/02699930441000238.

Valorie Burton is the bestselling author of nine books on personal development, including *Successful Women Think Differently* and *Happy Women Live Better*. She is the founder of The Coaching and Positive Psychology Institute, providing tools and training that build resilience, well-being, and productivity for life and work. Learn more at ValorieBurton.com.

Successful Women *Think* Differently

Popular author and professional certified coach Valorie Burton knows that successful women think differently. They make decisions differently. They set goals differently and bounce back from failure differently. Valorie is dedicated to help women create new thought processes that empower them to succeed in their relationships, finances, work, health, and spiritual life. With new, godly habits, women will discover how to

- focus on solutions, not problems
- choose courage over fear
- nurture intentional relationships
- take consistent action in the direction of their dreams
- build the muscle of self-control

In this powerful and practical guide, Valorie provides a woman with insight into who she really is and gives her the tools, knowledge, and understanding to succeed.

Start Here, Start Now

Stuck in a rut financially? Hanging on to a relationship you know is doomed? Wanting to start a new career but wondering if it's too late? It's never too late to learn that *being* stuck doesn't mean you have to *stay* stuck! Change happens one action at a time, one day at a time. Let Valorie spur you on to real transformation in the five key areas of your life—professional, financial, relational, physical, and spiritual. She will help you

- make small but meaningful changes—starting today
- conquer distractions and obstacles on your path
- fulfill your God-given purpose

Get Unstuck, Be Unstoppable

Using wisdom from God's Word and the principles of positive psychology, Valorie will help you make major life changes, take risks, and find the joy you've been searching for. You have the power to change your life—starting today!

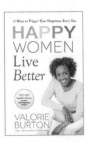

Happy Women Live Better

Valorie's warmth and encouragement will resonate with followers old and new, inspiring you to take hold of the abundant life God has in store. With a focus on relationships, career, finances, and physical and spiritual health, Valorie gently coaches you through the steps to find the happiness you desire.

To learn more about Harvest House books and
to read sample chapters, log on to our website:

www.harvesthousepublishers.com

HARVEST HOUSE PUBLISHERS
EUGENE, OREGON